Cambridge Monographs in African Archaeology
65
Series Editors: John Alexander and Laurence Smith

Safeguarding Africa's Archaeological Past

Selected papers from a workshop held at the School of Oriental and African Studies, University of London, 2001

Edited by

Niall Finneran

BAR International Series 1454
2005

Published in 2016 by
BAR Publishing, Oxford

BAR International Series 1454

Cambridge Monographs in African Archaeology 65
Series Editors: John Alexander and Laurence Smith

Safeguarding Africa's Archaeological Past

ISBN 978 1 84171 892 7

© The editor and contributors severally and the Publisher 2005

Typesetting and layout: Darko Jerko

The authors' moral rights under the 1988 UK Copyright,
Designs and Patents Act are hereby expressly asserted.

All rights reserved. No part of this work may be copied, reproduced, stored,
sold, distributed, scanned, saved in any form of digital format or transmitted
in any form digitally, without the written permission of the Publisher.

BAR Publishing is the trading name of British Archaeological Reports (Oxford) Ltd.
British Archaeological Reports was first incorporated in 1974 to publish the BAR
Series, International and British. In 1992 Hadrian Books Ltd became part of the BAR
group. This volume was originally published by Archaeopress in conjunction with
British Archaeological Reports (Oxford) Ltd / Hadrian Books Ltd, the Series principal
publisher, in 2005. This present volume is published by BAR Publishing, 2016.

Printed in England

PUBLISHING

BAR titles are available from:

              BAR Publishing
              122 Banbury Rd, Oxford, OX2 7BP, UK
EMAIL   info@barpublishing.com
PHONE   +44 (0)1865 310431
FAX   +44 (0)1865 316916
              www.barpublishing.com

In Memoriam

Ray Inskeep

Figure 1.1. Map of Africa showing the main areas considered. Numbers refer to chapters (see contents below): 1: Zimbabwe, Tanzania, Kenya; 2: Ethiopia; 3, 4: Nigeria; 5: Morocco, Algeria, Libya; 6: Mali; 7: Lesotho

Acknowledgments

This one-day workshop was convened at the suggestion of the then director of the University of London's Centre of African Studies, David Anderson; the editor wishes to record his gratitude to Dr Anderson, and also wishes to acknowledge the work of the Centre's secretary Jackie Collis, who efficiently and untiringly secured the necessary room bookings and organised the extensive publicity (emails, web and mail shots) that resulted in a very healthy attendance. The workshop could not have functioned so efficiently without the efforts and the logistical backing of the CAS. Thanks are also owed to my co-organiser Andrew Reid (University College London), and Edwin Johnson (SOAS) who provided extensive logistical help on the day. The following individuals also presented papers on the day, and the organisers wish to record their gratitude for their impressive contributions, some of which sadly did not make it in to print for varied reasons (a fuller discussion of the conference itself is presented in the editor's foreword): Sekhou Berte (University College London), Ms Maitseo Bolaane (University of Oxford), Patrick Darling (African Legacy/University of Bournemouth), Charles Gore (SOAS), Alberto Larocca (University College London), Kevin MacDonald (University College London), Peter Mitchell (University of Oxford), Mohammed Mohammed (independent scholar), Innocent Pikirayi (University of Zimbabwe), Andrew Reid (University College London), Alinah Segobye (University of Botswana), and Geoffrey Tassie (University College London). For their kind and efficient help with the publication of these proceedings, I would like to thank Dr John Alexander and Dr Laurence Smith (University of Cambridge).

Contents

Niall Finneran
Introduction 1

1. Shadreck Chirikure
   Cultural or Physical Survival? A Note on the Protection of
   Archaeological Heritage in Contemporary Africa 7

2. Niall Finneran
   Problems and Possibilities in the Protection of Archaeological
   Landscapes. The Ethiopian Experience in a Wider Context 11

3. Charles Gore
   A Question of Value: Nigerian Museums 17

4. Neil Brodie
   An Outsider Looking In: Observations on the African 'Art' Market 23

5. Alberto Larocca
   Conservation of Rock Art in the Sahara 27

6. Kevin MacDonald
   A Personal Perspective on Ethics and the African Archaeologist 33

7. Peter Mitchell
   Managing on Scarce Resources: The Past Record, Present Situation
   and Future Prospects of Archaeological Resource Management in
   Lesotho 37

8. Geoffrey Tassie
   Egyptian Cultural Heritage: Let's Work Together 47

Niall Finneran
   Epilogue 55

Contributors

Neil Brodie is the director of the Illicit Antiquities Research Centre, University of Cambridge and the editor of its journal *Culture Without Context*. He has written extensively on the illegal trade of portable artefacts.

Shadreck Chirikure hails from Zimbabwe, and is a doctoral candidate at the Institute of Archaeology, University College London, where he is engaging on research on the Southern African Iron Age.

Niall Finneran was formerly a British Academy Postdoctoral Research Fellow in the Department of Art and Archaeology, SOAS, and is currently lecturer in archaeology at Southampton University.

Charles Gore teaches African art history at the Department of History of Art and Archaeology, SOAS, University of London. His research focuses upon modern Nigerian artists, and he is himself a practising artist, drawing his inspiration from his work and travel in west Africa.

Alberto Larocca is a PhD candidate at the Institute of Archaeology, University College London, where he is currently researching Saharan rock art.

Kevin MacDonald is a senior lecturer in African archaeology at the Institute of Archaeology, University College London. He has worked extensively in Mali, and has recently begun work on African diaspora archaeology in the southern United States of America.

Peter Mitchell is lecturer in African archaeology at the University of Oxford and fellow of St Hugh's College. He has worked extensively on the prehistory of southern Africa, and has recently completed *The Archaeology of Southern Africa* (Cambridge University Press 2002).

Geoffrey Tassie is an Egyptologist and PhD candidate at the Institute of Archaeology, University College London. He has excavated widely in Egypt, and has been the driving force behind the establishment of the charity the *Egyptian Cultural Heritage Organisation* (ECHO).

INTRODUCTION

Niall FINNERAN

Writing of the Elgin Marbles in the Guardian newspaper on January 19th 2004, the Italian classical archaeologist Salvatore Settis noted that the recent signing of the Munich Declaration by 30 museums, while framing a strategy for the clampdown on illegal antiquities' trafficking, advised that no works of art should be repatriated if those works were taken before any relevant legislation existed; in his words "this implies that history, with all its stratifications, is preferable to the 'return to origin' idea of repatriation at all costs". An interesting and provoking thought, and especially so in the African context where obviously no legislation of any form hindered the colonial-era plunderers, looters and adventurers. It is arguable that we could speak, for instance, and in the same context of the case of the Elgin Marbles, of any legal niceties allowing for the ownership of say the Benin Bronzes or Ethiopian tabots; the British General James Napier, at the head of his rescue column in the Ethiopian highlands of the 1860s, and being very much a product of the antiquarianism of the time, did not feel that had to negotiate the purchase of such items. He just took them.

The case of the Ethiopian tabots (which are small, wooden slabs symbolising the Ark of the Covenant) rather encapsulates the wider and depressing tale of African antiquities held 'out of context'. An ethical point is obviously raised here; possession of the tabot is important for the church (both community and building), and maintains the holy symbolism of the place; their presence confers an act consecration. Arguably they are of little aesthetic merit; this is why the majority of the Napier Collection of Ethiopian 'ethnographic' material is held in the rather anonymous and inaccessible store in Hackney rather than under the bright lights and excited gazes of the British Museum's customers. So why not give them back? Or I am being too naïve? Perhaps, but we cannot go on clinging to that outmoded and ill-advised fall back position that 'they would not be cared for so well as they are here'. In the case of Ethiopia, this is clearly not true. A manuscript seized by the Napier expedition in the 1860s, and since 'lost', turned up (even though the Ethiopians generally knew of is whereabouts) under a secure glass display case in an Addis Ababa church, no concerns there about the ability or professional expertise of the Ethiopians in caring for this treasure.

There is, however, an ominous 'but'. Depressingly we read often of thefts within the formal museum structure of certain western African countries. In many cases museum workers augment their meagre salaries by providing goods from 'shopping lists' furnished by corrupt middle men or politicians at the behest of western collectors. A thorny issue indeed, and something of a catch-22 situation. Ideally we should like to return important material, it looks good, in the post-modernist, global village sense of responsible and ethical museums praxis (e.g. Knapp 1996). This material is 'only' of aesthetic or scholarly value to us, but is removed from the symbolic context of the artefact in its own setting. But even if we set minimum standards of care and conservation in its 'home' setting, it is still possible that the artefact will then be 'lost' and find its way on to the international art market (a point forcibly discussed by Patrick Darling, of which more later). So why bother? This is all part and parcel of a notional 'biography' of an object, a shift in meaning and context across time (e.g. Peers 1999), from fetish, to curio, to scholarly resource to fetish again, albeit financial rather than loaded with implicit symbolic meanings.

We should care. The past is not just the past of, say, a farmer from Benin, nor a west African, nor an African. It is a shared past of us all - again a very post-modernist interpretation and one which obviously justifies the retention of African objects by western Museums. The whole *raison d'être*, to return perhaps to the 17th century, and arguably the original roots of the British Museum, and as alluded to by the famous collector and traveller John Tradescant and his 'magazin of all manner of inventions': a place founded for the benefit of the knowledge of mankind, a post-enlightenment-era global village (Macgregor 1989). This is all fine for us, the western consumer. We can have these superb resources, a one-stop shop for us to visit on a rainy afternoon, or to fill more space on GCSE history projects. We can feel part of this global village, but the African consumer cannot. They are disenfranchised. One could hardly see the British Museum handing over some choice pieces of Anglo-Saxon art to an African museum to help them create a 'magazin of all manner of inventions' for their consumers. Imagine, just for a minute, being able to view prehistoric European, Classical, Egyptian material in an African museum. At the end of the day this is all a monstrous hangover of European colonialism, it will never happen, our attitudes do not allow it, but I would like to think that perhaps one day -- given the best efforts of those of us who profess to be one-world archaeologists and make our livings this way -- that African school children might be able to access, at first hand, some of the cultural treasures that formed the idea of

England, or France, or Greece, and be able to critically appraise the variety of human culture without recourse to the internet or the printed page.

Old habits, then, die hard. We must, as archaeologists and scholars of 'otherness', be able to at least be *seen* to act self critically and reflexively (e.g. Leone *et al.* 1987), being aware of our cultural perspective, almost promoting a hermeneutic approach to the study of African culture in the widest sense, continually reassessing, aware of the 'baggage' that we bring to the table, so to speak (Johnson and Olson 1992). I would like to think that gatherings such as these are part of the process, and anyway would have been unthinkable even twenty years ago. Just take a look at the Proceedings of the varied meetings of the Pan African conferences down the ages to see how far we have come. Occasionally, in between detailed papers on new forms of stone tool industry, types of pottery, finds of domestic animal bone, one might have been lucky to have found a brief mention of some aspect of conservation, or latterly cultural resource management (a key issue in the developing economies of the newly independent African states).

It only recently that we have seen whole sessions of these conferences (and those too of the Society of Africanist Archaeologists) devoted to numerous themes in this connection. One of the contributions offered here, for instance (Mitchell) reflects one of the best attended sessions of the 2000 SAFA conference at Cambridge: 'Dam Archaeology', organised by Fekri Hassan and Steven Brandt, which drew attention to the salvage archaeology possibilities afforded by the widespread construction of water-storage programmes in Africa; the flooding of vast tracts of land demanded landscape archaeology programmes of immense magnitude and resolution, as was seen in the then unprecedented UNESCO sponsored work in Nubia prior to the filling of Lake Nasser in the 1960s. Given the sort of money we are talking about, it is possible to mobilise large numbers of international experts (in the case of Nubia in the '60s many of these teams were 'brought off' with the promise of some share in the materials; it is of the author's own opinion that in future any such work should see the construction of dedicated and large museums to hold the material, within the host country, but this is a digression), conservation strategies (even to the point of removing large standing remains, where they exist), and of course publication, both academic and popular, preferably in multi-lingual and multi-media formats. Responsibility, direction and above all a sense of working together will help -- so too will the injection of vast amounts of money. This then is a very brief and rather subjective and personal appraisal of the key issues facing African archaeology with regard to 'safeguarding Africa's past'. A brief overview of the contributions, presented below, will show the sheer scale and variety of the problems that beset us.

Neil Brodie's piece clearly draws upon his wide knowledge of the murky world of the international illicit antiquities' markets, and he would be the first to admit (rather sadly) that being director of the University of Cambridge institution that seeks to highlight these issues he comes across such cases, on the global scale, far too often. Here some of the more outrageous crimes are brought to light, crimes that sadly show very entrenched mindsets and often an inability (driven by sheer acquisitive greed) to even attempt to control the market. In an ideal world, he suggests, the African problem could be remedied by getting more archaeologists out onto the ground and helping train the locals in good management-practice techniques. Sadly (and quite rightly) he observes that Africa tends to be rather low on the list of exotic archaeological research priorities, many archaeologists are attracted elsewhere, to better funded areas.

The editor, as an active African archaeologist, with experience of training field archaeologists from many countries, can only agree with such sentiments. One would suggest, given the relative scales of funding generated by postgraduate students from their varied countries of origin, that per capita there are far more western-trained Japanese or Saudi archaeologists and art historians than African ones. The appalling economic dynamics that govern the way the Universities are forced to find money here in the UK, for instance, militates against the inclusion and training of students with obvious potential whose sole weakness is to come from a country that lacks the financial clout to pay for them. In short, we come back to money again, and until the continent of Africa (sub-Saharan at least) begins to yield vast quantities of oil or other mineral wealth we will not see the scale of indigenous African academic involvement in the UK academic archaeology scene. The relative numbers of MA students from Africa versus those from Japan and the Middle East in archaeology programmes in the UK reflect this dichotomy of haves and have-nots. It is even more sobering to reflect, whilst we are mentioning access and visibility, how many Africans are represented in lecturing positions in the UK across all subjects.

Shadreck Chirikure, a Zimbabwean national, presents a heart-felt plea, and a very obviously personal piece highlighting his concerns, with reference to the Zimbabwe situation in particular but within a wider eastern and southern African context. Let us try, for a minute, to empathise, and imagine that we are trying to raise a large family on a minimal income perhaps in the shadow of a monument where, so we have been told, it is possible with a few hours' digging at night to obtain objects of some value that could be sold off in the nearest city to provide enough food to keep a family for a while. If we had not been educated about the value of such a monument, then we would surely not hesitate to fetch the shovel. Even if we had, the economic situation is so harsh that we would probably say 'so what'. Again, it comes to making obvious value judgements, and back again to the catch 22. As the author points out, when governments have to trim wage bills, it is often the museum staff or antiquities service that bears the brunt. This has happened in Zimbabwe, even though President Mugabe has shown himself to have at least some sensitivity as to what should constitute a 'represented past' even if he did not recognise the ramifications of this idealised past (see Ucko 1994). These wage cuts not only provoke unrest among museum staff and encourage low morale, they also leave a number of important sites at risk and unguarded. Additionally, the museums staff in such situations may be tempted, as is the case in Nigeria, to apply their knowledge to pursuing the darker arts of antiquities trafficking.

Niall Finneran looks at the possibilities and protection strategies for historic landscape conservation, the case study here being the UNESCO world heritage site of Aksum, Ethiopia. Whilst an important addition to this list of international cultural treasures, it is clear that the bestowal of such an accolade actually has very little financial implications. There are no legal requirements to treat the conservation of a UNESCO WHS any differently from any other block of landscape, and most importantly direct grants from UNESCO for landscape protection are rare. As we go to press, the author has learnt of a European Union-funded project to kick-start the tourist infrastructure of Aksum. Whether this has any knock-on effect for improving the museum display facilities, signage, landscape management or monument conservation remains to be seen. The author here offers a strategy, based on UK local government practice, that may begin to help manage and conserve the landscape and more importantly to present it in the best possible way.

Charles Gore's piece accurately portrays one of the continent's real horror stories: the looting of Nigerian museums. Gore tackles the key issue of the relevance of the objects to the modern peoples of the area; does this in some way diminish claims to such works of art? Could we draw an analogy with the potential for repatriation of human bone material, especially such material that is obviously temporally and spatially far removed from the associations of the modern inhabitants who demand its return? This is obviously a thorny issue. Again, it seems that the best way to ameliorate the problem is to throw money at it. Enhanced training schemes are desirable, but on the other side of the coin, Gore argues, western museums should be aware of their own responsibilities. He cites the procedures followed by the Horniman Museum in South London, and their dealings and consultations with the Oba of Benin.

Alberto Larocca considers the threats to the magnificent corpus of Saharan rock art. As an artistic and aesthetic resource, this art is hugely valuable in contextualising the history of human representation, yet paradoxically it is this beauty – both inherent and within its landscape situation – that presents the greatest threats. Tourism to the region has recently increased after a period of political instability, and these sites are becoming the focus of extensive tourist activity. Larocca argues for a strategy for sensitive and sustainable eco-tourism. It is clear that attracting and charging western tourists can, in the right circumstances, help make up any potential shortfall in the budgets of national antiquities' councils. Such measures have already worked well in Egypt and in Kenya, for instance, albeit on different types of site.

Kevin Macdonald's very personal and reflective memoir proposes some practical ideas that he has found particularly helpful during his extensive research work in Mali. This approach is embracing and geared towards maximum involvement of local people, both in terms of training and education, yet characteristically the emphasis is also upon being self-critical. How, for instance, are archaeologists perceived, are they regarded as being treasure hunters, looters, exploiters rather than scientific researchers excavating under controlled and measured conditions with no perception of financial reward for what they find. Far too often it seems that we, as archaeologists in another country, do not take enough time to take into account the feelings and perceptions of the communities within which we are working; we cannot then afford to cultivate an 'us' and 'them' approach. Such a strategy for being 'self-reflexive' has been followed by Ian Hodder at Çatal Hüyük in Turkey; there he seeks to maximise participation and in a very post-modern way allow for a multiplicity and equal validity of interpretations. Accessibility and inclusiveness, for instance, is helped by an extensive web-site containing video recordings of the reactions of locals and excavators alike to the site (see web reference: http//catal.arch.cam.ac.uk/catal). Granted, the project happens to be exceptionally well funded, but are such imaginative schemes beyond Africanist archaeologists? Additionally MacDonald makes the telling point that on occasions we may be guilty of applying double standards:

> 'Local groups who value their past are less likely to let harm befall its vestiges. Would villagers at Avebury stand mutely by while someone came along with a lorry and started carting off the stones?'

This emphasises a core theme running through these contributions; to paraphrase a recent UK election promise: 'education, education, education'. (As a brief aside and editorial note, the villagers of Avebury, as recorded by William Stukeley in the seventeenth century, did not require outside help to destroy their stone circle. They did it themselves fairly effectively!)

Peter Mitchell considers how in the case of a very small African country (Lesotho), it has been possible to conduct a wide-ranging and effective environmental impact programme tied to research needs (I do think it important, especially here in the African context, and because it clearly exists, to emphasise this seemingly artificial dichotomy between 'research' led and 'salvage' excavation). Mitchell points out that although the legislation for antiquities protection is well developed, financial constraints limit the effectiveness of such strategies. Storage and display problems exist, as do limited funds for effective publication and outreach, although it must be said that the general tone of the paper is optimistic.

The final paper presented here, by Geoffrey Tassie, tackles on a very wide scale the threats posed to Egypt's rich wealth of cultural material. As a whole, CRM strategies and legislation in Egypt is fairly well developed; the Supreme Council of Antiquities happens to be headed by an effective and very single-minded scholar in the shape of Zahi Hawass, and the balance of power has clearly shifted from the old and rather traditional 'colonialist' mentality that the western archaeologists and scholars clearly knew best. Tassie's paper outlines the key threats to Egypt's past, and sketches in the circumstances behind the foundation of the Egyptian Cultural Heritage Organisation (ECHO), and then outlines some ideas – drawn mainly from UK legislation – for helping manage and classify archaeological landscapes.

The author of the piece (Tassie) has for some years been interested in developing strategies for teaching advanced excavation methodologies in Egypt to Egyptian students, and it is high time that African archaeology as a whole woke up to the fact that methods more suitable to Wheeler's excavations at Maiden Castle in the 1930s, whilst not being acceptable as good practice in the UK today, should also not be regarded as being acceptable ways to excavate Africa's past. Good research practice, whilst encompassing educational strategies and outreach, should not ignore the one key area where perhaps we have taken an active and direct part in damaging Africa's past for good: the act of hurried and poorly-recorded excavation.

This then is a very personal account and overview of my readings of what is presented here; here, stripped bare, are horror stories, tales of deceit, genuine mistakes, problems of under funding, poor infrastructure, political paralysis and in some cases uninterested academics. These narratives and analyses seem depressing, but the fact that we can air them so openly can only be a good thing. We can begin to act, and must do so multi-laterally. At the end of this can we begin to offer some solutions? We talk at length about responsible practice, education and more education, awareness but at the end of the day the ultimate cost of safeguarding Africa's past can only be paid in US Dollars and Euros.

How then can we achieve this? We have the goodwill and we have, for the most part, the strategies. Many countries have adequate legislation in place; at this end, Europe and the west, the illicit antiquities trade is fairly well legislated for, but how well policed it is is a different matter, as a Southampton student pointed out recently it is regarded as being something of a 'white collar crime' yet it largely continues unchecked, as does the destruction of African heritage. Can we envisage a more enhanced and developed role for UNESCO, a cultural version of the UN Blue Helmets perhaps, a centrally-funded team of archaeologists and conservators with real power to act? Can large sums of money be found to fund an enlarged programme of training of museums personnel and technicians across Africa? Or is this all ultimately doomed by the global imbalance of wealth and power? There is no holy grail, but what we have here, on the small scale, is a sample of ideas, sound practical approaches to the problem that seem to have worked in part and in varied degrees in different situations across the continent. These ideas may be broadly framed as follows on the basis of the papers presented here. In a sense here is our attempt at an outline charter. I think it combines, effectively, sound practical and methodological approaches. They just require money and goodwill.

- There should be some provision for a centrally-administered UNESCO budget to be used as an emergency fund in the most severe cases. Such money would be used to fund emergency conservation measures rather than infrastructural development. Backing this up would be a pool of conservation and archaeological expertise -- almost an archaeological rescue team -- that could be called upon at short notice to undertake any rescue measures. Such a strategy obviously works on the macrocosmic scale, i.e. site and archaeological landscape protection.

- Within African governments, specialist funds from UNESCO sources or World Bank to be set aside to encourage the development of templates for sustainable and responsible tourist strategies. This should be done, if at all possible, in liaison with national and international tourist groups. Only tourist companies signing up to charters guaranteeing their participation in the overall responsible tourism strategy to be allowed access to sites. In all cases local guides to be used, employed from the local community and being made aware of their responsibilities as custodians and educators. Any damage to the site will directly affect the income to the local community, even resulting in site closure. It is not generally desirable, we suggest, to physically erect barriers and restrict access to sites unless absolutely necessary.

- Archaeologists must, as part of their permit award criteria, undertake to engage in a widespread education campaign, not merely send a local translator out to have a chat in the odd village hall.

- Archaeologists to be aware of good fieldwork practice, recording and need to publish site reports in a variety of media and languages to heighten accessibility. If archaeologists do not feel themselves to be competent in training locals in *advanced* excavation techniques (especially single context recording, surveying and digital mapping) they should employ somebody competent to do this. In my experience it is desirable (and often fairly easy) to employ a UK-based contract field archaeologist from a county unit or private contractor. These workers are the best trained field archaeologists in the world and their expertise on a variety of sites is without parallel. I would argue that it is worth the investment.

- More specifically states need to develop dedicated National Monuments' Records (NMRs) in order to inventory and assess the state of existing sites and maintain a database for researchers and developers. If archaeologists are granted permits for excavation, it should be made a requisite that they undertake intensive survey in their concession zone (using GPS and not compass/pedometer!) and undertake to tie these data into the NMR. Such surveys must be multi-period, even if the excavation, for argument's sake, is focusing upon ESA material. We can afford the luxury of picking and choosing our sites, but we must be aware of our responsibilities as trained personnel to the wider strategy of CRM.

- Finally, in terms of the approach to the artefact rather than larger-scale site, landscape or heritage, we must police more stringently that 'white collar crime' that is illicit antiquities trading. It still is not taken seriously.

These are some suggestions for a way of progressing, but on a final and personal note, I do feel that the situation is improving, albeit slowly, yet depressingly one can envisage conferences on safeguarding Africa's past being relevant for many years to come.

References

Johnson, H. and B. Olsen (1992). 'Hermeneutics and archaeology: on the philosophy of contextual archaeology' *American Antiquity* 57/3: 419-36.

Knapp, B. (1996). 'Archaeology without gravity: post-modernism and the past' *Journal of Archaeological Method and Theory* 3: 127-158.

Leone, M., P. Potter and P. Shackel (1987). 'Toward a critical archaeology' *Current Anthropology* 28/1: 283-302.

Macgregor, A. (1989). '"A Magazin of all manner of inventions". Museums in the quest for "Salomon's House" in seventeenth-century England' *Journal of the History of Collections* 1/2: 207-212.

Peers, L. (1999). 'Many tender ties: the shifting contexts and meanings of the S. BLACK bag' *World Archaeology* 31/2: 288-302.

Ucko, P. (1994). 'Museums and sites: cultures of the past within education – Zimbabwe, some ten years on'. In *The Presented Past: Heritage, Museums and Education* (Stone, P. and B. Molyneaux eds.), London: Routledge, pp. 237-282.

1. CULTURAL OR PHYSICAL SURVIVAL? A NOTE ON THE PROTECTION OF ARCHAEOLOGICAL HERITAGE IN CONTEMPORARY AFRICA

Shadreck CHIRIKURE

INTRODUCTION

As the curtain fell on the twentieth century, many archaeologists were optimistic that the new millennium would finally see the effective management and protection of archaeological sites all over the world. In that light, numerous master plans which were geared towards the effective protection of archaeological heritage in Africa were formulated. It was hoped that with new strategies and approaches developed on the continent – by Africans and for Africans -- the destruction of African archaeological sites would end (see Schmidt and McIntosh eds. 1996 *passim*). However, a few years into the new millennium, an overview of the situation reveals that the protection of archaeological sites on the continent remains ineffective, to the extent that some archaeologists could argue that these sites can never be effectively protected, and the situation has been exacerbated by the political and economic ills that are afflicting the continent. The key problem is this: as long as these severe economic conditions exist, then, sadly, measures against the destruction of archaeological sites receive a very low priority. A number of examples are discussed here and serve to illustrate the problem.

African governments faced with problems such as the shortage of basic economic resources, disease, and famine often prioritise the provision of basic services for the physical survival of the people. Thus 'cultural' survival through the protection of archaeological heritage is often seen as an unnecessary drain on a country's meagre resources, and is not regarded as being a priority. Faced with the ravages of drought, and unemployment the general public has resorted to employing every tactic to earn a living. Regrettably, this quest for survival has led to the plunder of archaeological heritage in search of antiquities or precious minerals. With such a labyrinth of problems bedevilling the effective protection of archaeological sites in Africa, as archaeologists how can we lobby governments and the public to provide for the protection of sites? In this contribution, it is argued that the only way of achieving cultural survival in such a life-threatening situation is to integrate archaeological heritage in mainstream development through the medium of sustainable cultural tourism. Proceeds from such a process can then be used to protect sites as well as catering for the provision of basic infrastructural facilities necessary for 'physical' survival. There are some cases in Zimbabwe, Mali and South Africa where archaeological heritage has been utilised in a way that benefited society economically and thus ensured the long term survival of such sites.

PROTECTION OF ARCHAEOLOGICAL SITES: AN OVERVIEW

Archaeological sites are irreplaceable resources. In order to keep this invaluable inheritance from antiquity for posterity, we have attempted to devise a variety of ways of protecting them from destruction (Pearson and Sullivan 1995 *passim* for an overview). Protection refers to almost everything done either on site or off-site to prolong the life of archaeological sites, at the highest level this would include the gazetting of sites, framing of legislation and the setting up of administrative structures, while at a lower level it includes the imposition of physical barriers, the restoration/conservation of disintegrated parts of the monument/site and basic maintenance activities on site. Ideally, a policy on the protection of archaeological sites designed at a higher level ensures unity of purpose and co-ordination between the two levels. In this respect, there are laws and administrative bodies that were established in virtually every African country to protect archaeological sites from destruction. Examples of these are the National Museums and Monuments of Zimbabwe (CAP 25:11) which also established a body to look after the sites in trust for the public. In Botswana the Monuments and Relics Act 1970 was designed to achieve the same end. In most African countries, national museums and antiquities departments are responsible for the day-to-day upkeep of sites as well as doing research to document unknown ones, and they are also responsible for maintaining inventories of sites that exist in a country. Thus in principle, African countries have the necessary laws and administrative structures in place to effectively protect archaeological sites. However, a critical look at the prevailing situation shows that the ideal is often short circuited owing to a lack of resources which renders them incapable of effective protection of archaeological sites. It is all very well having effective legislation – from a water-tight legal point of view – but having the capability to enforce these laws of the ground is quite another matter. The key variable is, unfortunately, economic.

SOCIO-ECONOMIC AND POLITICAL PROBLEMS AND THE PLUNDER OF ARCHAEOLOGICAL SITES. THE CASE OF ZIMBABWE

Zimbabwe has been recently experiencing acute economic problems that have climaxed in runaway inflation in the last year or so. As a result of the curtailment of international finance due to internal political problems, the government has increasingly found itself with little resources and income (Mlambo and Pangeti 2000 *passim*). As such it has embarked on a programme to cut spending on 'luxuries', and regrettably this included a reduction in government spending on museums -- which in its view did not contribute to direct income generation and this had disastrous consequences for the body tasked with heritage protection. With a reduction in government funding, the National Museums and Monuments of Zimbabwe found itself with a shortage of resources and capacity to effectively protect archaeological sites (Ndoro and Pwiti 2001). In terms of the National Museums Act, archaeological sites in the country are divided into two categories: 'national monuments' i.e. those special sites embodying specific scientific and social values and 'ordinary sites' which are judged as being less significant. The antiquities legislation stipulates that national monuments must be visited routinely by inspectors of monuments who would then conduct condition surveys and other maintenance activities. Also, archaeologists are tasked to conduct inventories to document new sites in the course of their survey. Owing to the twin problems of lack of resources and shortage of staff, the National Museum is failing to protect archaeological sites in the country to the extent that even the higher-status national monuments are threatened with destruction. A witness to this is the plundering of the Zimbabwe tradition sites of Chiumnungwa in south western Zimbabwe (pers. obs.). A group of villagers formed a co-operative to mine gold at Chiumnungwa and the surrounding areas. The activities of the treasure hunters of the late 19th and early twentieth centuries were still in some peoples' minds and as such they illegally dug tunnels on the site in search for gold; from the villagers' perspective, the gold was invaluable in generating income for them to survive. Unfortunately, for the site, the mining activities went on for over six months leading to the loss of tons of cultural material without any contextual documentation. In its defence, the National Museums argued that the lack of financial resources plaguing its budget planning, and the resultant loss of capacity, meant that the available monuments' inspectors were incapable of inspecting archaeological sites in their respective regions. Its not surprising that the illegal mining ventures were brought to the attention of the National Museums of Zimbabwe by a South African archaeologist who had brought his students to the site (Ndoro and Pwiti 2001).

CULTURAL RESOURCE MANAGEMENT IN TANZANIA AND KENYA

By way of comparison, we now turn to eastern Africa where again we see how the curtailment of Governmental budgets set aside for the management of cultural heritage translates into direct damage of archaeological sites and monuments. In its attempt to save revenues, the Tanzanian government often finds itself with little money to spare for heritage resource management, and activities such as the protection of archaeological sites are perceived as a waste on the state's already strained resources. As such, museums lack the capacity and staff to look after archaeological sites. According to Mturi (1996), there are too few trained antiquities officers to cover the wide variety and number of archaeological sites in Tanzania. A number of cases may be cited here: despite being one of the most spectacular rock art in the region, there is no protection given to the rock art of Kondoa because of lack of resources (Mabulla 1996). Cases of illegal excavations on rock shelters by people looking for treasure are numerous, and other cases of simple, wanton vandalism have been reported (Felix Chami pers. comm.). In Kenya, the government is desperate to provide for key social services, and again the scarcity of economic resources is one of the chief reasons that archaeological sites are destroyed (Kusimba 1996). In this light, it is argued that providing services like hospitals is important in comparison to protecting economically-useless relics from the past. A good example is the destruction of the site of early Mombassa by the government of Kenya. The construction of a hospital, in Fort Jesus, accidentally recovered remains of the earliest occupation at Mombassa, instead of inviting archaeologists to conduct an impact assessment; the government ordered construction to go ahead since in its opinion rescue operations would have delayed the provision of a key social service (Kusimba 1996). In a similar vein, as the country struggles to modernise and develop its infrastructure, archaeological sites have been decimated in the process. In this case, the development of beaches along the coast of east Africa has resulted in the extensive destruction of Iron-age 'Swahili' sites. Here we have a case of irresponsible tourist infrastructural development.

ILLICIT TRADE IN CULTURAL PROPERTY IN WEST AFRICA: THE CASE OF MALI

We may gain another perspective on the problem by considering what is happening across the continent in Mali. Like many other African countries, Mali is plagued by poverty, and in order to survive, many local communities have capitalised on the illicit trade in cultural property in as far as they clandestinely excavate sites for terracotta to sell to international art dealers (Brent 1996). The discovery of ancient terracotta in the 1970s has brought international attention to the Inland Niger Delta. As a result, international art dealers have collaborated with local communities in plundering sites for the pieces of art. The local communities burdened with starvation and unemployment often see this as an opportunity to earn a living (Sidibe 1996); they organise themselves into teams and plunder the sites for antiquities. The looted pieces often find their way in the Western world where the terracotta is in demand. An inventory conducted in the late 1990s showed that 80% of the sites in the Inland Delta of Mali were looted and plundered for terracotta (Sidibe 1996). Although a museums infrastructure does exist, it lacks the economic capacity to look after sites and as a result they are often unable to stem the looting. As Brent (1996) has argued, the illicit trade in antiquities poses the greatest threat to archaeological sites in West Africa as opposed to eastern and southern Africa where arguably an artistic tradition of aesthetically desirable ancient sculpture is not present.

COPING WITH CONSTRAINTS: PATHWAYS TO THE EFFECTIVE PROTECTION OF ARCHAEOLOGICAL SITES IN AFRICA

With the socio-economic and political problems currently experienced in Africa, as outlined above, how can archaeologists lobby governments and the public alike to protect the sites and remind them of their responsibilities? One of the lasting solutions to this is the use of archaeological sites as key economic resources in cultural tourism. Proceeds used from programmes of responsible and sustainable tourism can then be used for the physical survival of people and in promotion of a sustained heritage protection strategy. In this way, the only way of achieving cultural survival through the protection of archaeological sites is to use them for the benefit of society. The case of Djenne in Mali is an illuminating example. Located in the Inland Niger Delta, the site has been plundered by treasure hunters who mainly came from of the impoverished local communities (Sidibe 1996). In order to halt the damage caused by looters, archaeologists in Mali decided to involve local communities in the protection of the sites, as well as promoting the sites as a centre piece for cultural tourism. Local communities were allowed to sell curios to tourists so as to generate revenue. Augmented by educationnal awareness campaigns, the integration of Djenne into mainstream development has significantly reduced cases of clandestine excavations and local communities who were formerly villains are now championing the protection of archaeological sites (Kevin Macdonald pers. comm.). Turning to Zimbabwe, the country witnessed episodes of aimless vandalism on many archaeological sites, which climaxed with the smearing of oil on the rock art site of Domboshava (Pwiti and Mvenge 1996). Faced with such vandalism, the National Museums of Zimbabwe realised that it was important to use archaeological sites as an economic, revenue-generating resource. As such, it embarked on a programme of opening the sites for tourism and involving local communities in the process. In the case of Domboshava, the National Museums called for a stakeholders meeting at the national monument of Domboshava in which all interest groups met and deliberated on issues of mutual concern. In the end the local community was given back its traditional custodial rights at the site, while the national museums remained the legal custodian. It was also agreed that the archaeological sites in the Domboshava area were to be used for the benefit of the local community. As a result, the site was promoted for tourism and in addition to selling curios, local people formed dance groups to entertain the tourists, thus generating considerable income in the process. Now, local people who had viewed the archaeological site as being a source of revenue saw it in a different way. Also, people from the area were employed as tour guides and interpreters at the site, which brought an element of community ownership in the whole process. For its part, the National Museums of Zimbabwe is taking the case of Domboshava as a success story, and has since applied it to other sites like Silozwane and Old Bulawayo where local people are involved in the protection and selling of curios at sites. In South Africa, using archaeological sites as economic resources has been adopted with great success in protecting the site of Thulamela (Miller 1996). In the reconstruction of the site, burials were discovered and project managers involved local people in the project. When the site was opened for tourism, it rapidly became a real success story and the case of Thulamela is often cited as one successful model of integrating archaeology within tourism for the benefit of all stakeholders (Ndoro and Pwiti 2001); this is so because local people sell their curios to tourists and their traditional dances add to the attraction at the site. It can be argued that archaeologists must protect sites in a way that benefits local communities, and in that way archaeological sites can be effectively looked after for future generations. Coupled to a programme of concerted community involvement, the use of archaeological sites as economic resources through the promotion of cultural tourism is proving to be a viable option of looking after archaeological sites in these times of straightened financial circumstances.

As demonstrated in this paper, the integration of sites into tourism strategies is one way (though by no means the only one) of achieving long-term survival of archaeological sites. This is in as far as the use of archaeological sites for tourism purposes generates money which can be ploughed back into protecting the sites; the cases of Domboshava in Zimbabwe, Thulamela in South Africa and Djenne-Jeno in Mali have shown this approach to be highly effective in protecting archaeological sites for future generations. However, in view of the elitist nature of archaeology as a discipline in many African countries, such an approach ought to be complemented by educational awareness campaigns to educate the public on the importance of looking after archaeological sites. By emphasising the fact that these sites are not necessarily an economic drain and given the right circumstances can work to be viable financially, both for the local community and national government, we can go some way towards removing the many threats that face Africa's heritage. It just needs imagination and work to make a success of it.

References

Brent, M. (1996). 'A view inside the illicit trade in African antiquities'. In *Plundering Africa's Past* (Schmidt, P. and R. McIntosh eds.), London: James Currey, pp. 63-78.

Kusimba, C. (1996). 'Kenya's destruction of Swahili cultural heritage'. In *Plundering Africa's Past* (Schmidt, P. and R. McIntosh eds.), London: James Currey pp. 201-224.

Mabulla, A. (1996). 'Tanzania's endangered heritage: a call for a protection program' *African Archaeological Review* 13: 197-214.

Miller, S. (1996). 'Rebuilding the walls of sixteenth-century Thulamela'. In *Aspects of African Archaeology* (Pwiti, G. and R. Soper eds.), Harare: University of Zimbabwe Publications, pp.837-8.

Mlambo, A. and E. Pangeti (2000). *The Zimbabwe Economy, 1930s to the 1990s*. Harare: University of Zimbabwe Publications.

Mturi, A. (1996). 'Whose Heritage? Conflicts and contradictions in the conservation of historic structures, towns and rock art in Tanzania'. In *Plundering Africa's Past* (Schmidt, P. and R. McIntosh eds.), London: James Currey, pp. 151-160.

Ndoro, W. and G. Pwiti (2001). 'Heritage management in southern Africa: local, national and international discourse' *Public Archaeology* 2/1: 21-35.

Pearson, M. and S. Sullivan (1995). *Looking after Heritage Places: the Basics of Heritage Planning for Managers, Landowners, and Administrators*. Melbourne: Melbourne Press.

Pwiti, G. and G. Mvenge (1996). 'Archaeologists, tourists and rainmakers: problems in the management of rock art sites in Zimbabwe'. In *Aspects of African Archaeology* (Pwiti, G. and R Soper eds.), Harare: University of Zimbabwe Publications, pp. 817-24.

Schmidt, P. and R. McIntosh (eds.) (1996). *Plundering Africa's Past*. London: James Currey.

Sidibe, S. (1996). 'The fight against the plundering of Malian cultural heritage and illicit exportation: national efforts and international co-operation'. In *Plundering Africa's Past* (Schmidt, P. and R. McIntosh eds.), London: James Currey, pp. 79-86.

2. PROBLEMS AND POSSIBILITIES IN THE PROTECTION OF ARCHAEOLOGICAL LANDSCAPES THE ETHIOPIAN EXPERIENCE IN A WIDER CONTEXT

Niall FINNERAN

Some of the contributions presented in this volume have inevitably focused on the value (often monetary) of the artefact, or moving up the spatial scale to the protection of the archaeological site. This contribution widens the scope further, and considers the totality of the archaeological heritage within its culturally and naturally constructed stage: the landscape. Landscape archaeology *sensu lato* is an obvious buzz-word today; over the last few years archaeologists have moved away from the narrow scope afforded by site-based archaeology towards a consideration of the wider cultural context. The landscape is an important factor (Gramsch 1996; Stoddart 2001 *passim*) and it too is deserving of careful conservation. This paper looks at the experience of archaeological landscape management from an Ethiopian perspective, with special reference to the World Heritage Sites of Aksum and Lalibela, but also seeks to place these examples within a wider context with a comparison with the well-known and much debated landscape management plans presented for the Stonehenge archaeological area in southern England. This is not to imply, from a quasi-neo-colonial perspective, that British is necessarily best; the UK has made many mistakes in this regard to be held up as a shining paradigm, and the process of arriving at a satisfactory legislative framework has been painful (Darvill 1987 *passim*; Wainwright 1989). The goal of this contribution is to highlight key issues in archaeological landscape management and to propose how they might be adequately tackled. Before considering the sites in question, let us put the concept of the archaeological landscape under the microscope.

DEFINING SPACE AND ARCHAEOLOGICAL LANDSCAPES

Archaeologists have been slow to recognise the potential of the wider world beyond the excavated area. We have moved on from simple concepts of site catchment analysis, and have accepted a broad holistic approach where we can emphasise spatial and temporal control (Crummley and Marquant 1990; Dennell 1987), although we must be aware of the limitations of our data (Johnston 1998), we can stretch our horizons and perceive how the archaeological data, once a vital, living medium, was meant to be viewed within the landscape, how sites were approached, what they offered, even we do not go as far as Christopher Tilley's phenomenological approaches to accessing perceptions of space in the past (Tilley 1994 *passim*). Within the African context, landscape study often means regional survey, itself either a locational tool for potential sites for future excavation, or, and most importantly, a means of viewing the wider picture form admittedly problematic surface data (Bower 1986). The most important thing to recognise is that landscape archaeology (or basically survey) is a cost-effective tool, and as sites are noted and described, we can also 'bolt on' a programme of cultural resource management assessment. Why stop at ascribing the site to a certain period when we can take the data a step further and assess proactively the nature of potential threats to this newly discovered site? In this respect, we can begin to construct a sites and monuments register, much as is used (successfully) in assessing developmental strategies and developer-led/rescue archaeology in the UK (more of this later).

Geographical Information Systems can help in bringing our archaeological landscape to life, as well as assisting in assessing threats to these sites. G.I.S. is a cost-effective tool for the archaeologists, and its use has become widespread in cultural resource management (Savage 1990). There is no excuse any more for ignoring the attractions of building a comprehensive G.I.S. digital archive that, circumstances permitting, can be utilised by archaeologists and developers in African countries. The Archaeological Data Service, based at York University in the UK, advises applicants for Arts and Humanities Research Board (AHRB) grants on the suitability of their digital archive, and have produced excellent guides to good practice which must be adhered to by all grant awardees (Gillings and Wise 1998 *passim*). The application of overlaid data layers, which may incorporate aerial photographs, vegetation survey and geophysics results is an invaluable tool for defining the archaeological landscape and building strategies to conserve it (Wheatley 1995); this has already been highly effective in Scottish archaeology, for instance (Murray 1995). This then is the broad framework for studying, analysing and quantifying the archaeological landscape. Before considering the African data, let us examine the context of archaeological landscape management from the British perspective, and consider the management of perhaps the most famous British archaeological landscape of all.

THE STONEHENGE WORLD HERITAGE SITE AND BRITISH LEGISLATIVE CONTROLS

The primary conception of a World Heritage Site (WHS) does, by its name, imply perhaps an unhealthy preoccupation with the site rather than surroundings, although the following discussion emphasises the whole landscape, a factor now clearly enshrined in the overall Stonehenge management plan (Wainwright 1995 and pers. comm.), and now more broadly recognised with the foundation in 1985 of the International Committee on Archaeological Landscape Management (I.C.A.L.M.) (Biörnstad 1989). UNESCO created the WHS concept in 1972, defining the criteria for selection as being sites of 'outstanding universal value' (UNESCO 1972), and at the time of writing there are some 630 designated multi-period sites worldwide regarded as satisfying these basic criteria. Further criteria for selection, defined under 1999 revised regulations, state that sites should: "represent a masterpiece of human creative genius; exhibit an important interchange of human values over a span of time, and bear a unique or at least exceptional testimony to a cultural tradition that has disappeared" (UNESCO 1999). The selection of these sites is often hit and miss, and at no point is any financial assistance or prioritising of conservation emphasised; in the UK, at least, this factor has lead to problems (Evans *et al.* 1994). In short, we seem to be left, as Evans *et al.* suggest, with a beauty pageant devoid of any pragmatic and proactive plans for conservation and protection.

Stonehenge and its immediate landscape seems to have suffered particularly, and it was the tourist-led pressure upon this landscape that has led to the development of a landscape management plan that certainly may be regarded as a useful template for similar strategies within the UK (Geoffrey Wainwright pers. comm.). English Heritage's (2000) comprehensive master plan seeks to address a number of key 'values': archaeological significance, spiritual values, tourism values and research and understanding values. It may be useful here to amplify the value quantification, especially in relation to the two key Ethiopian sites discussed here later. These ideas have been clearly articulated by Tim Darvill (1995), who recognised the clear need to accommodate the wishes of all interested parties. Darvill usefully defines three value stages that should be considered within the framework of a management plan: use value reflects acts of consumption, tourism, research, education and local economics; option values reflect the emphasis on production rather than consumption, where the landscape is viewed as a resource for the future, finally the existence value, the most nebulous factor, refers to the importance of the resource for group identity, or to put it loosely the potential 'feel good factor'. These concepts have clearly been borne in mind by the planners of English Heritage.

The key aims of the Stonehenge landscape management plan seek to strike a balance between the interested parties and their part in the schema of the value system. The obvious objectives as set out in the report seek to increase public awareness in the site, develop a sustainable approach that balances needs of access, conservation and farming (it is a living, working landscape) and seeks to identify economic and cultural benefits of the WHS in partnership with the local community. The active conservation strategy ensures both the physical survival of remains, but crucially seeks to enhance the visual character of the landscape setting. The last concept (set out in objective 9, English Heritage 2000: part 4 p. 11) is best embodied in the plan to close the nearby A344 road and return it to pasture, and perhaps most excitingly tunnel the busy A303 beneath the immediate archaeological landscape. Now visitors will be able to approach the monument through its landscape as it was meant to be approached when it was built, along the Avenue, and indeed enter the stones without hearing the background noise of nearby traffic. This is an exciting and imaginative step, but will necessarily entail a reduction in visitor access as the new visitors' centre and parking will be some 2 miles away in Amesbury. The knock-on economic effects for the local community will also be profound, although the plan seeks to spread the economic benefits around the wider landscape. This plan represents the culmination of years of planning and consultancy, but it should not be regarded as the finished article as it seeks to evolve as local circumstances change. In the UK at least, landowners and developers are now bound by strictly defined controls, even if on the global level the significance of the WHS may be reduced to the beauty pageant level. The impact of the Planning Policy Guidance Notes 15 and 16 (Department of the Environment 1990), has led to a degree of protection for archaeological sites that has served as a legislative paradigm across Europe. Developers now pay for necessary archaeological investigations on sensitive sites. Here are just a few points that could be adapted on the broader scale. We will now depart from the downs of southern England and consider the situation at two of Ethiopia's key UNESCO World Heritage Sites: Aksum and Lalibela (see fig. 2.1).

Aksum, located in the northern Ethiopian highlands, is known as the centre of the Aksumite polity that dominated the region during the first eight centuries AD, and which enjoyed wide trading links with Nubia and the eastern Roman world. From an archaeological perspective, immediate attention is drawn to the magnificent range of monolithic stelae, tomb complexes and large 'palace' structures, but these individual sites, which make up in amalgam the WHS designation (defined in 1980), represent only the tip of the archaeological iceberg. Recent research here (e.g. Phillipson 2000; Fattovich *et al.* 2000), utilising extensive survey and excavation has uncovered a range of archaeological material from the Early Stone Age upwards. In popular imagination, however -- and here we may recall Darvill's value criteria -- the focus is upon the stelae, but the town, although geared towards the little western tourism that comes its way, also has another, more vital living tradition. The cathedral church of Maryam Tsion is the centre of Ethiopian Orthodox Christianity, and as such the town has become a centre for pilgrimage and devotion for Ethiopia's large Christian community. More than any other factor, it is the annual cycle of ecclesiastical festivals that represent the economic lifeblood of the town. Meanings and symbols are everywhere, but this is also a workaday place; a large local agricultural community taps

Fig. 2.1. Map showing location of Aksum in Ethiopia

into the pilgrim and tourist-orientated economic dynamic. There are strains upon the archaeological landscape everywhere, but demands need to be balanced with the needs of the local community.

From early sources such as Enno Littmann's 1906 German Aksum expedition, we have gained a broad picture of the archaeological landscape, and it is instructive to see in their evocative pictures just how the character of the local landscape has changed over a century (see also Phillipson 1997). The first structured landscape study was initiated by Joseph Michels in 1974 (Michels 1988), and this study, which largely focused on the area to the south and northwest of the town, is still an effective cornerstone for understanding the wider landscape dynamic. Recent work by the author (Finneran 1999) sought to build on Michels' data, and when taken with the results of the 1993-7 British Institute in Eastern Africa work (Phillipson 2000) and the ongoing work by the joint American-Italian team (see especially Ogundiran 1995), we have begun to build the foundations of what could be a really effective and comprehensive sites and monuments database for the surrounding region. (It should be noted that Ethiopian antiquities' legislation permits work only within a 10-kilometre radius of the town. As such, we do not have the definitive picture of the wider Aksumite landscape system).

This sites and monuments database still only exists in disparate publications, but steps are being taken to integrate these data more efficiently and certainly in digital archive format (Fattovich *et al.* 2000). It is to be hoped that this comprehensive database will be available not just at local and national antiquities level, but also to the local planning department. Having followed the ideals of the UK PPG 16 legislation, with the reference to extensive, local archaeological site data, we should step a little further and consider how a programme of rescue archaeology can be built in on top of the broader programme of landscape characterisation and assessment. Much archaeological work at Aksum has been research-driven. I do not wish to draw an artificial dichotomy between salvage, or rescue, archaeology and research excavation, but this is how the picture is dominated. Aksum is a living town. The demands of tourism have resulted in a burgeoning of hotel-based development, certainly towards the southern end of the town, and the demands of the growing population has resulted in the construction of large reservoirs in the locality. There is an obvious need for salvage archaeology here. This is not a totally alien concept; when the Yeha hotel was being built in the mid 1970s an archaeological team was able to investigate two shaft tombs on the site. More recently, in 1995, the present author was asked by the Aksum municipality to investigate two garden sites earmarked for development within the town, setting, it is hoped, a happy precedent for future work. The author was also able to investigate the area around the Filfili reservoir complex in the same year, but these were isolated occurrences. The fact that an active archaeological team was present in the town permitted a degree of rescue investigation that would never normally have been undertaken. In recent years the situation has improved in Ethiopia as a whole; work continues on the sites for reservoir development and road building (Steven Brandt pers. comm.) and in Aksum itself recent salvage archaeology and assessment work has started to begin in advance of road construction (Tekle Hagos pers. comm.), something never considered by the occupying Italians in the late 1930s when they drove a road through the site of the important palace of Ta'akha Maryam!

The creation of a sites and monuments register is a very real possibility for the near future, especially given a degree of European Union investment, and allied to a growing development of rescue-based archaeology; we will have laid the foundations for a comprehensive landscape management plan. There are, however, other issues requiring response. The standing archaeology itself, the vital sub-component of the wider landscape character, is also under threat. These concerns have been addressed by Rodolfo Fattovich's comprehensive assessment of the Aksum archaeological area (Fattovich *et al.* 2000). The stelae, the obvious tourist focus, would not appear to be at risk from natural or cultural factors (this is especially important with stelae 3, see Phillipson and Hobbs 1996), but the subterranean tombs present special problems, and some form of visitor control may be required in order to maintain the natural environment in the tombs (a similar consideration is discussed by Tassie (this vol.) in relation to the Kings' Valley, Egypt). This is a problem with the tombs of Kaleb and Bazen, which are the most accessible tomb structures for the visitor, but is especially difficult with the recently excavated Mausoleum and Tomb of the Brick Arches complexes in the Central Stelae Park. Carefully covered and sealed at the end of each excavation season, it is possible that if and when these fascinating structures are eventually opened to tourists that there could be a degree of structural deterioration through sheer numbers of visitors. Buildings conservation advice has, it should be noted, formed a key component in the overall B.I.E.A. research strategy, and it is hoped that a more intensive future programme of buildings recording and risk assessment will form the core of any future concerted research efforts at Aksum. This is especially desirable with post-Aksumite buildings, including the relatively modern examples of vernacular Tigray buildings in Maleke (Old) Aksum and the residence of the Nebura-Ed.

The actual character of the landscape too can conspire against the survival of archaeological material. Around the hill flanks, the predominant soils are the thin red lithosols, normally unfavourable for cultivation, and with a propensity to wash off the hillsides. It is only by careful maintenance of terracing and the planting of eucalyptus that the soils can hold fast; otherwise they would wash off and cover surface archaeology. The intensive agricultural system of the region may place demands on these soils, and result in further erosion episodes. In addition, the ploughing of the vertisolic complexes of the valley floors has the potential to disturb archaeological site signatures (e.g. Steinberg 1994), although the local *marasha* plough only has a small plough bit resulting in about 15 cm penetration of the topsoil (pers. obs.). Plough damage is therefore not a realistic factor in the destruction of local sub-surface archaeology. Fattovich's scheme for a management strategy for the Aksum region largely addresses the key problems discussed above (Fattovich *et al.* 2000: 55), although there are other components subsumed within the plan, and the generalised site inventory (Fattovich *et al.* 2000: 59-67) represents a worthy attempt at the framework for a sites' and monuments' register (and see table 2.1 for a general risk assessment to sites).

It is perhaps because Aksum has been relatively well archaeologically investigated that the basic frameworks and strategies for landscape conservation and management have been put in place. This situation, however, is not reflected at the WHS of Lalibela in the Lasta highlands of Wollo, some 200 kilometres to the south-east of Aksum. During the 12th century AD, the town of Lalibela became the political focus for the usurpers of the Solomonic dynasty, the Zagwe. Here, in the heartland of the Agaw peoples, King Lalibela built a capital essentially modelled on Jerusalem. Here is a transplanted sacred landscape; even the small and unremarkable watercourse running through the town was named the Jordan River to reflect this ideal of a new Jerusalem. Over a period of many years a number of monolithic rock-hewn churches were constructed, in the eyes of the 17th century Portuguese traveller Alvares some of the most remarkable structures in the world. It is this cluster of architecturally superb and unusual rock-hewn churches that has primarily won the accolade of WHS (1978) for what is a bucolic and sleepy little town. Unlike Aksum, there has been little co-ordinated archaeological work here. There has been no regional survey, and as such the churches are seen as isolated sites, rather than integrated components of the Zagwe socio-economic system. Ethiopian historiography emphasises this point; the emperor traditionally lived in large, mobile encampments according to legend, and as such the special nature of Lalibela as a unique and solely ecclesiastical centre is emphasised.

Lalibela as a town suffers from the twin pressures of pilgrimage and tourism, although perhaps not to the extent seen at Aksum. Hotel development places a major strain on the archaeological landscape, but here the emphasis centres on the church as a site rather than a consideration of the wider landscape picture. Conservation efforts are directed solely at the individual churches. Bolstered by European money, the treasuries of the buildings have been meticulously recorded, and architectural advisors seek ways in which to arrest the deterioration of building fabric and wall paintings alike. Incongruous sheet-metal roofing, supported by long eucalyptus poles now enclose the major churches, helping keep the elements from further damage to the roof (especially noticeable at the church of Geneta Maryam, where the north-eastern corner has markedly deteriorated), but doing little to enhance the overall

Table 2.1 Archaeological sites in the Aksum Landscape: spatial and temporal patterning and evaluation of risk from destruction

Chronological attribution	Approx dates	Types of site	Risk assessment
ESA/MSA	? 2.5 Myr. – c. 15 Kyr. BP	Open/single find spots	Erosion from primary contexts
LSA mode 4	? 15 Kyr.-9 Kyr. BP	Satellite functionally-specialised tool fabrication/butchery areas, population concentration around Gobedra.	Definite risk from agricultural works, possibly reservoir building. No urban likelihood.
Mode 5 aceramic/ceramic phases	? 9 Kyr.-2 Kyr. BP	Open and rockshelter, and as above	Plough damage, reservoir construction, urban building
Pre-Aksumite	C. 800 BC-100 BC	Few recognised, probably small, non-nucleated farming settlements.	Difficult to define on the basis of small sample.
Aksumite	C. 100 BC-AD 800	Nested, multiple settlement typology, nucleated. High urban and rural populations in defined, functionally-specific areas. Manufacturing zones and defined elite/burial zones. Extensive re-use of pre-Christian sacred area. Formalised zonation of landscape.	High risk in urban zone, especially with building works. On the fringes a possibility of site damage. Tourism a key factor in the deterioration of the larger monumental sites. Also potential for agricultural damage.
Post-Aksumite-modern	C. AD 800 - AD 2000	Stark definition of town and country, farmstead is the key rural social and economic unit. Extensive site re-use in urban zone.	Not archaeological sites *per se*, but key buildings of historical interest at risk from tourism. Traditional vernacular architecture at risk

perspective of the actual building within its landscape context. Recent reports suggest that an Italian architect has proposed enclosing the churches within a plastic dome, *à la* Greenwich (Girma Elias, pers. comm.); again careful consideration of the visual impact of the church within its landscape rather than an isolated, individual site is of extreme importance. As things stand, Lalibela effectively lacks an archaeological landscape to manage; if funds directed towards individual church restoration and conservation (obviously a very worthy goal) could be selectively diverted to a wider archaeological study, then we would be in a better position to define conservation priorities and meet the challenges posed to a site like this as Ethiopia gradually re-opens for tourism. It is a most unusual case that this Ethiopian WHS has seen so little focused archaeological consideration.

We have made a start in Aksum, and given the right funding conditions, similar foundations may be put in place at Lalibela, but how do we take the next step? We could perhaps frame any strategy in regards to our series of Darvill's value criteria as adopted by English Heritage. In terms of use value, we need to recognise that the archaeological resource acts on many levels; in terms of research strategy, local economics and indeed education. Obvious direct issues would be the continued training of local workers, broader enhancement of local awareness -- perhaps underpinned by a concerted effort to develop and improve Aksum's museum facilities. Our option values recognise the future production potential. The integration of local economic needs with the overall management plan is paramount, and consultation should include all local landowners, state, private and church. In this way the foundations of effective management zoning can be put in place; for effective control the landscape management plan would call for sub-delegation of day-to-day responsibility. Responsible and ethical archaeological research strategies for the future need to be discussed, and preferably archaeological areas directly threatened by development should receive priority. Finally, arguably more than perhaps any other WHS in the world, Aksum represents a special spiritual place, a town of totemic significance for Ethiopia's Christian community. Any future management strategy needs to take these issues into account. The plan presented by the Fattovich team (Fattovich *et al.* 2000: 85-90) rightly emphasises a multi-disciplinary approach, and largely gets to grips with most of the key problems. There are a few reservations on this author's part, however, especially in regards to building a depositional map utilising coring techniques, a worrying lack of local consultation in the overall framework and indeed no discussion of how to enhance the archaeological landscape where this may be allowed.

It is to be fully emphasised here that the foregoing observations are very much personal in nature. The economic situation of Ethiopia itself stands in the background, shadowing over these grandiose concepts for archaeological management strategies. The international community needs to help, not just in terms of the obvious financial support, but also in terms of effective training and education. A re-assessment of the beauty contest role of the WHS is also long overdue. The Stonehenge archaeological management plan is itself the result of years of planning and British Government funding beyond the education budgets of some developing countries. It is a useful template that if not copied in its entirety, could be abridged and adapted to suit the needs for other countries. I fully accept that Ethiopia, as with many other countries in the world, has a problem in regards to the traffic of portable antiquities, and in this regard the money spent on cataloguing ecclesiastical treasures (a key black market money earner) is money well spent, as indeed is the programme of building conservation, but I think this is too narrow a view in the longer term. We must move away from period-specific, site-focused perspectives and see the wider picture. The landscape is the natural backdrop to the whole drama; the integrated picture needs to be understood.

References

Biörnstad, M. (1989). 'The ICOMOS International Committee on Archaeological Heritage'. In *Archaeological Heritage Management in the Modern World* (Cleere, H. ed.), London: Unwin Hyman, pp. 70-8.

Bower, J. (1986). 'A survey of surveys: aspects of surface archaeology in Sub-Saharan Africa' *African Archaeological Review* 4: 21-40.

Crummley, C. and W. Marquant (1990). 'Landscape: a unifying concept in regional analysis'. In *Interpreting Space: G.I.S. and Archaeology* (Allen, K. et al. eds.), London: Taylor and Francis, pp. 73-80.

Darvill, T. (1987). *Ancient Monuments in the Countryside: An Archaeological Management Review*. London: English Heritage Archaeological Report 5.

Darvill, T. (1995). 'Value systems in archaeology'. In *Managing Archaeology* (Cooper, M. et al. eds.), London: Routledge, pp. 40-9.

Dennell, R. (1987). 'Geography and prehistoric subsistence'. In *Landscape and Culture: Geographical and Archaeological Perspectives* (Wagstaff, J. ed.), Oxford: Blackwell, pp. 56-76.

Department of the Environment (1990). *Planning Policy and Guidance Note 16*. London: Department of the Environment.

English Heritage (2000). *Stonehenge World Heritage Site Management Plan. A Summary*. London: English Heritage.

Evans, D., J. Pugh-Smith and J. Samuels, (1994). 'World heritage sites: beauty contest or planning restraint?' *Journal of Planning and Environmental Law* June 1994: 493-576.

Fattovich, R., K. Bard, L. Petrassi, and V. Pisano (2000). *The Aksum Archaeological Area: A Preliminary Assessment*. Istituto Universitario Orientale : Laboratoria di Archeologia working paper 1: Naples.

Finneran, N. (1999). *Post-Pleistocene Socio-Economic Developments in the Northern Ethiopian/Eritrean Highlands: A Case Study from Aksum, Tigray*. Unpublished PhD thesis, University of Cambridge.

Gillings, M. and A. Wise (eds.) (1998). *The Archaeological Data Service G.I.S. Guide to Good Practice*. Oxford: Oxbow Books.

Gramsch, A. (1996). 'Landscape archaeology: of making and seeing' *Journal of European Archaeology* 4: 19-38.

Johnston, R. (1998). 'The paradox of landscape' *European Journal of Archaeology* 1/3: 313-325.

Michels, J. (1988). 'The Axumite Kingdom: a settlement archaeology perspective'. In *Proceedings of the Ninth International Conference of Ethiopian Studies* (Gromyko, A. ed.), Moscow: Nauka, pp. 173-183.

Murray, D. (1995). 'The management of archaeological information -- a strategy'. In *Computer Applications and Quantative Methods in Archaeology 1993* (Wilcock, J. and K. Lockyer eds.), Oxford: BAR Publishing. British Archaeological Reports International Series 5598, pp. 83-7.

Ogundiran, A. (1995). *A 1995 Archaeological Reconnaissance in Aksum, Northern Ethiopia. Perspectives on Aksumite Settlement Geography and Material Culture*. Unpublished report submitted to the Social Science Research Council, Boston, August 1995.

Phillipson, D. (1997). *The Monuments of Aksum*. London/ Nairobi; Addis Ababa: British Institute in Eastern Africa; Addis Ababa University Press.

Phillipson, D. (2000). *Archaeology at Aksum 1993-1997*. London/Nairobi: Society of Antiquaries of London/ British Institute in Eastern Africa Monograph.

Phillipson, D. and D. Hobbs (1996). 'Is the Aksum standing stela in danger?' *Journal of Ethiopian Studies* 29: 1-8.

Savage, S. (1990). 'G.I.S. in archaeological research'. In *Interpreting Space: G.I.S. and Archaeology* (Allen, K. et al. eds.), London: Taylor and Francis, pp. 22-32.

Steinberg, J. (1996). 'Plough zone sampling from Denmark: isolating and interpreting site signatures from disturbed contexts' *Antiquity* 70: 368-392.

Stoddart, S. (ed.) (2001). *Landscapes from Antiquity*. Cambridge: Antiquity Papers 1.

Tilley, C. (1994). *A Phenomenology of Landscape*. London: Berg.

UNESCO (1972). *Convention Concerning the Protection of the World Cultural and National Heritage*. Paris: UNESCO.

UNESCO (1999). *Operational Guidelines for the Implementation of the World Heritage Convention (Revised)*. Paris: UNESCO.

Wainwright, G. (1989). 'The management of the English landscape'. In *Archaeological Heritage Management in the Modern World* (Cleere, H. ed.), London: Unwin Hyman, pp. 164-70.

Wainwright, G. (1995). 'Concluding remarks'. In *Stonehenge in its Landscape* (Cleal, R. et al. eds.), London: English Heritage Archaeological Report 10, pp. 493-4.

Wheatley, D. (1995). 'The impact of information technology on the practice of archaeological management'. In *Managing Archaeology* (Cooper, M. et al. eds.), London: Routledge, pp. 163-174.

3. A QUESTION OF VALUE: NIGERIAN MUSEUMS

Charles GORE

There has been much debate about the role of the museum as an institution in Africa and how it may best serve the various communities in which they are located (Ardouin and Arinze 1995 *passim*; 2000 *passim*). One focus of this debate has been the ways in which local, national and regional cultural heritages are constructed dependent on the preservation of the material remains of the past. Cultural heritage is a complex, if diffuse, term which conceptually embraces a range of (sometimes conflicting or contested) ways in which these material remains are utilised to contribute to present day agendas and particular interpretations of the past. This can be in terms of nation building, the construction of local and regional identities (including ethnicity) as well as presenting alternative, sometimes radical, counter interpretations of history or new readings of the landscape to mention but a few of the possibilities. Material remains are especially important in Africa, as Schmidt and McIntosh (1996: xi) note, because many of the actual historical trajectories of communities and societies within the continent "are not accessible through documentary record" and the recuperation of these societies has to rely on material remains, cultural artefacts and oral traditions. Consequently artefacts and, as importantly, the record of their stratigraphic situation offer a key, and sometimes the only means of understanding these communities and societies as they have developed within local and regional trajectories over time. The looting of such material artefacts from their archaeological sites and the loss of the stratigraphic record, in the worst case scenarios, erases from recorded history knowledge about entire communities, societies and the agency of the individuals who formed them. For this reason much of the current debate about the roles of museums in Africa is dependent upon preservation of the past without which their possibilities as institutions, whether potential or realised, and are thus severely limited in what they can offer to communities, other collective groupings or the nation state. Conservation of artefacts, and indeed prevention of their illicit extraction and appropriation, should be a primary concern of the museum as an institution.

Questions have been raised about the responsiveness of national museums in serving local communities compared to the opportunities afforded by local museums that are run and financed independently from the nation state (Konare 1995). In the dialogue with local interests and agendas these museums perhaps offer more scope to mobilise the community in safeguarding local archaeological sites from illegal excavations. However local independent museums still operate within nation states and depend on their infrastructures in a similar way to nationally funded museums. The illicit extraction and transportation of artefacts across national boundaries highlights the importance of the sovereign nation state as the key means of intervention in preventing these activities, using a range of institutions which include, among others, the judiciary, the museums and the police (and other enforcement agencies) within its boundaries. Moreover when artefacts have evaded border controls, it is the nation state which makes representations to other nations (where the artefacts may now reside) and to supra-national organisations such as UNESCO, with its 1970 Convention on Illicit Traffic. Consequently national museums have a key role to play in monitoring such predations and in coordinating their curtailment with both other institutions within the nation state and in linking up with comparable institutions in other countries. Without the infrastructure of national museums, local and community museums have great difficulty in regulating flows of illicit artefacts beyond their immediate locality. Both Arinze (1995) and Ardouin (1995) stress a potential lack of resources available to community museums and this also may hinder their institutional capacity to intervene effectively in preventing this traffic (albeit that they may be highly effective in monitoring and preventing such illicit activity within a particular community or locality).

In considering the reasons for the legal and illegal exportation of artefacts from African countries, it is a truism that they have greater monetary value in Western markets. Moreover, in many countries in Africa and in particular Nigeria, (which forms this case study), there has been a serious economic decline since economic *Structural Adjustment Programs* have been applied, whether imposed or voluntarily accepted as in Nigeria in the late 1980's. This has increased the relative value of this illegal export trade. As part of SAP programs there has been an ensuing shift of resources from state institutions to the informal sector which has weakened these state infrastructures in the long term, most visibly perhaps in the decrease in value of salaries due to the presence of acute inflation of, in some years, more than 100% inflation. This has been accompanied at certain times by delays in payment of wages by up to six months. It also has resulted in difficulties in maintaining the quality of museum buildings and in the conservation work that can be achieved on such limited and depleted budgets. In the competition for resources, the National Commission for Museums and Monuments in Nigeria must take its turn in the priorities of the nation state, particularly as its economic productivity in financial terms is negligible compared to other ministries such as oil (or in other terms of criteria such as national security as maintained by the army or police). In response to these circumstances, some heads of station of particular Nigerian museums in the late 1990s have used their initiative and ingenuity to engage in partnerships with civil society to generate desperately needed income in the form of the hiring out of facilities and space for a range of purposes such as corporation conventions, sponsorship launches, Pentecostal rallies and other ways -- in fact comparable to the fostering of corporate sponsorship by Western museums.

However, despite these local efforts, museums in Nigeria are especially vulnerable at all levels of personnel from local attendants to conservators to heads of station. Their value is not prominent in the order of things, especially in a declining economy. It is therefore little wonder that the plentiful cash flow generated by the illicit trade in artefacts provides a potent means of circumventing the efforts of museums to prevent, or at least hinder, illegal extraction and removal of cultural artefacts. This is often compounded by the remoteness of cultural heritage as a salient concept to local populations that may view it more as an available resource to be exploited. An example of this is demonstrated in the demand for land that has intensified in Benin City as it has expanded in the last two decades of the 20th century. Houses have encroached on the Iya -- the historic earthen ramparts that encircle various areas of the city -- despite their status as a public and national monument. Here local conceptualisations of cultural heritage view it as a resource to be exploited and consumed rather than preserved (pers. obs.).

The very ways in which cultural heritage has been constituted as museum practice is shaped by the disciplinary trajectories of archaeology in America and Europe and their relations to specifically Western notions of nationhood, the past and identity. These have been adopted and shaped by a burgeoning leisure industry that is part of the service economy of Western countries. Such constellations of cultural heritage have to be rethought and reconfigured to meet African aspirations, needs and requirements. This is a challenge that African museologists address in their ongoing practice and long term goals. They are however hindered in realising these goals by the economic constraints under which they operate. All the while the illicit removal of artefacts and the (mass) destruction of stratigraphic contexts destroy the bedrock for understanding Africa's past (McIntosh 1996).

The development of the 1970 UNESCO Convention on Illicit Traffic (Prott 1996; O'Keefe 2000) provides an international framework to regulate, monitor and police the international illicit trade in artefacts. It allows the Western purchasers of these artefacts to be held to account, although as Corbey (2000) notes this accountability is still fluid, negotiable and subject to circumvention. However the ultimate value and demand of these illegal artefacts is generated by Western purchasers and this process itself highlights the complex interrelationships between their local extraction and sale within global economic networks. The UNESCO Convention provides a clearly defined framework and protocol for dealing with the illicit trade in cultural artefacts but this continuing trade also appears to generate ambivalent responses on the part of Western museums in identifying and taking action in relation to the various components of these global networks.

In many ways these responses are in part constituted by the historical trajectories of museums and their relations to the history of colonialism. Many artefacts from non-Western societies were acquired by Western museums the 19th and early 20th century through methods that now seem at the least questionable by contemporary standards. Moreover the museum as an institution very much developed within this timespan as one of the means of displaying within a public space the ideological spectacle of colonialism (Coombes 1994). These histories also raise the current debate of repatriation in which the legitimacy of particular museums to retain possession of these artefacts is contested. Benin artefacts are a lively example of this debate[1], particularly as some of these artefacts are still relevant to ritual ceremonies carried out by the Oba of Benin and his palace officials up to the present day. However in seeking to condemn the sale of illicit cultural artefacts and not appear vulnerable to the claims of repatriation a certain disengagement with non-Western museums seems evident, corroborated by concerns over conservation issues relating to artefacts, lack of adequate security and a perceived general weakness or fragility of supporting infrastructures for museums. These issues pose important questions for the long term relationships between Western and non-Western museums. Moreover these questions are shaped by the challenge of how to encourage local and regional value in museums as institutions in Africa without which their institutional capabilities are undermined.

Posnansky (1996) offers a concise account identifying many of the problems posed and offers a number of pragmatic and concrete remedies. In brief he argues for the necessity of local initiatives which include the multidisciplinary training of African museologists so that they are able advocate the importance of conserving cultural heritage across disciplinary divides, their professional remotivation (in part through developing educational links with universities) and the development of apprenticeship schemes for the induction of new personnel. The curriculum of educational courses and professional training should be re-orientated to the specific present day needs and concerns within the Africa continent with provision of new courses, such as site management and site conservation. He further suggests that more outreach initiatives should be adopted to involve local communities more directly so that public awareness of the issues raised by cultural heritage. Similar initiatives to these suggestions have been developed and adapted to local circumstances. One such example is the way that Benin Museum, Nigeria,

---

[1] At the present time an exposition of the claims made on the Benin artefacts can be found at the African Reparations Movement website http://www2.arc.co.uk/arm/home.html.

has built up close relations with the brasscasting ward in Igun street[2] (for which Benin is internationally known) and acted as an advocate in successfully gaining government funding for the renewal and repaving of Igun street, which was completed in 2001. In terms of relationships with Western institutions Posnansky argues for stronger bilateral relations including long term strategic partnerships such as twinning arrangements where there is an exchange of expertise and training between Western and African institutions. Similarly multilateral co-operations have much to offer as the West African Museums Project established in 1982 has notably demonstrated, serving as a forum for regional issues and debates but also developing further forums of debate and professional linkages across the continent.

However with respect to initiatives set up by Western institutions, clearly local African and nation state agendas are never going to exactly coincide with Western agendas (and notions) of cultural heritage preservation. In supporting museum and other institutional infrastructures with Western resources, there may be some leakage of resources or appropriation due to different forms of economic organisation driven by local agendas and policies which may seem a digression, if not inimical, to Western assumptions of governance and accountability. There has to be an understanding in such collaborative projects of the different cultural and social ways of co-ordinating and achieving particular agreed outcomes to projects. It is important that such relationships of co-operation are based on dialogue rather than hidden but exercised relations of power over the intended beneficiaries. Western curators who utilise artefacts from African-based collections and museums often take an interest in the museums and personnel that they have contact with but these interactions often lapse once the exhibition or project is completed. The main beneficiaries at the end of these processes of exchange are the exhibiting Western museums who gain in cultural prestige and funding while little of long term value is gained by the donors. The networks provided through these contacts are often based on the personalised relations developed by visiting curators. Such personalised relationships do not provide a solid basis for long term or strategic relations between African and Western museums but rather construct transient and unequal networks of patronage and favour[3]. Few exhibitions which tour Western cities include in their itinerary cities on the African continent[4]. However it is crucial to maintain a dialogue and provide support for museum infrastructures through official long term partnerships at all levels and to provide access to global information networks. A good example of low cost, collaborative and long term support is the current posting and continued maintenance of a website onto the internet of the National Archives of Nigeria Enugu Branch by the Centre for Modern Oriental Studies, Berlin (http://www2.hu-berlin.de/orient/nae/:10/12/02). In this case there is the dissemination of the work and bibliographical indexes produced by U. O. A. Esse which highlights the resources provided by the National Archive at Enugu.

TWO CASE STUDIES

The Horniman museum in London has taken an interesting direction in developing a new exhibition space entitled 'African Worlds'[5] which opened in 1999. In displaying artefacts from their African collections, a focus of attention was how they constructed particular representations of Africa (Shelton n.d.). This was allied to a concern to reach the diverse audiences of south London where the museum is based, particularly communities shaped by the histories of the Black Atlantic. In seeking to engage with these communities, the role of these artefacts and their histories is open to interpretation (as evinced in repatriation debates) and it was considered incumbent on the museum to explore the competing claims to ethnographic authority if it was to meet the needs of its diverse publics (Clifford 1988 *passim*; Shelton n.d.).

In this exhibition development the museum creatively exploited the situation. It sought to incorporate and so 'democratise' these various competing claims and interpretations into the narratives of the museum display in both the presentation of artefacts and accompanying texts rather than define it through the sole ethnographic authority of a curator, legitimated by Western claims to a scientific knowledge and expertise. This it accomplished by setting up an advisory committee of curators drawn from the African continent and diaspora to suggest the relevant themes. This was accompanied by nine field projects in Africa and the diaspora with the brief of engaging in a dialogue with the artists and communities in which the artworks were commissioned, so that their voices could be included within the ethnographic narratives presented in the exhibition. An important aspect of these initiatives was also to provide educational support and co-operation with museum partners in Africa, so that within the framework of dialogue an exchange of information and resources took place rather than appropriation solely to the benefit of the Horniman museum.

Benin City was a particular focus of these efforts to reformulate museum practise and as Anthony Shelton notes:

> "The Benin collections had already been subject to various claims for repatriation by the African Reparations Movement, and are indisputably perhaps, the most controversial part of the Museum's holdings. It was clear that without confronting the problems these objects posed, the unequal relations between Africa and Europe, stemming from an antagonistic colonial

---

[2] This relationship however is not 'neutral' as brasscasters often depend on the export of their work both regionally and to other continents and, therefore require certificates from the museum confirming that these are contemporary works of art, not antiquities.

[3] Ironically this use of personalised networks is a criticism often directed at African states.

[4] South Africa is perhaps the main exception to this observation and this is perhaps due to particular history and its privileged links to Western economies.

[5] Indeed almost the whole museum has been redesigned and refurbished in an extensive programme.

history, which they had come to symbolise, it would be extremely difficult to build a successful new exhibition which would be acceptable as a celebration and testament to the achievements of Black Atlantic cultures." (Shelton n.d. : 2)

With the collaboration of the Director of the National Museum of Benin City Dr. J. Eboreime (who was also a member of the advisory panel), research in the field was conducted on the Benin plaques putting into practice the remit developed by the Horniman and its advisory panel. The National Museum of Benin worked with palace officials of the Oba of Benin with whom they have a longstanding relationship, particularly in regard to conservation advice and work carried out on artefacts at the palace. This allowed for a depth of explanation of the Horniman's Benin plaques drawn from the museum and palace institutions within Benin City and asserted their rights to interpret these depictions of past events, both locally and internationally[6]. At the same time the Horniman set up computer facilities with internet facilities to give the Benin museum access to global networks and further communication between it and the Horniman, including its web pages of the exhibition. A pilot educational project was also carried out. In some ways, working with the hierarchy of the palace officials at Benin City placed an emphasis on a single, centralised context of interpretation. It perhaps elided the possibility of contested claims and differing interpretations from other constituencies within Benin City. Moreover in providing seemingly historical narratives the information at the Horniman museum fails to flag to the interested viewer that these are present day interpretations of scenes of court life depicted at the palace of the Oba that were made some three to four hundred years ago (Picton 1997). These narratives are dependent on 20th century agendas and reinventions and as Akinola has shown such narratives have been subject to rapid change during this time (Akinola 1976) -- moreover the ruling dynasty was itself reconstituted by the British colonial administration in 1914 after an interregnum of 17 years. Indicative of this is that the plaque form, so highly prized in Western museums where they now reside, was for the most part discontinued in the seventeenth century. The plaques themselves were stored and not even on display when discovered by the British Punitive Expedition when it invaded Benin City in 1897. The Horniman museum perhaps has been more successful in opening out narrative voices of diverse communities with some of the other exhibits, such as the commissioned Ijele masquerade made specifically for the museum. However Shelton makes the important point that "Changes in the way museums exhibit the visual culture of other societies cannot take place independent of our cultural, political and economic relationships" (Shelton n.d.). These relations need to be critically and reflexively explored within exhibitions and in how they construct the field of display and its discursive formations, locally, regionally and between continents.

Clearly Western museums have many demands made on them and are subject to similar economic constraints and budgetary pressures as their colleagues in the rest of the world. In these circumstances it is perhaps too easy to ignore (or place a low priority on) an ongoing dialogue with non-Western museums. But with the movements of individuals across the world, the apparent distance or separation between artefacts located in the Western museum space and the communities which produced them (or who can lay claim to a common history) has collapsed (Harvey 1978 *passim*). This makes it incumbent on museums to engage in dialogue and reposition the role of museums if they are to justify their retention of artefacts from these different parts of the world. In developing their relations with these other parts of the world and, if long term strategic relationships are to be developed, these economic constraints which limit the capacity for Western museums to engage in dialogue need to be taken account of. Projects which seek long term dialogue also need to be low cost in contrast to the ambitious but high cost enterprises such a temporary exhibitions which gain one-off funding.

Consideration also needs to be given to whom the dialogue is directed at. It is easy to slip into a dialogue between elite scholars of different continents who share a common international idiom and can construct a common project, however it may play out in local terms and agendas (Hannerz 1989). Major benefits to dialogue would accrue if projects are directed at including the lower tiers of museum institutions. These are the institutional groupings who are often written out of the equation except through forging of personal ties with foreign academics on an individual basis as co-researchers or more likely research assistants. But these tiers are crucial to the maintenance and institutional reproduction of museums as sites for the development of value in cultural heritage. Projects directed at these tiers, or the very least to include them, would reinforce value in museum institutions as well strengthening their infrastructures. Moreover, in the design of such projects one needs to factor in local realities and expectations instead of assuming the mantra of complete accountability to Western funding institutions. Local expectations and dialogues are often quite different to the seemingly disinterested quest for knowledge of Western research. As a consequence there should be a certain expectation of manageable leakage to local agendas that is part of pragmatic approach to take account of local needs and conditions. However this is not an acquiescence in local malpractices (which can be found in any part of the world, although their guise may be quite different) but a negotiation and sensitivity to local practices and local forms of accountability (Gore and Pratten 2003).

I have tried to develop one such project with these pragmatic ideas in mind which was directed at ethnographers at Benin Museum in Nigeria. These are trained personnel who however have few or no resources to conduct fieldwork due to the extra costs that such projects entail (J. Eboreime Pers. comm. Benin City, 1998). Despite their training they are engaged in administration and/or coping strategies to survive in the weakened bureaucratic hierarchies in the context of a post

---

[6] There is a copious literature on the Benin artefacts, most of which is based on secondary sources rather than direct research in the field, leading to a constant recycling of Western paradigms of art historical interpretation with the attendant superimposition of Western presuppositions.

SAP (structural adjustment programme) nation state. A frustrating situation at best, and one that it potentially destructive to the museum infrastructures, both in economic terms and in the loss of morale of personnel within the museums. This low cost partnership proposal focused on ethnographers through the implementation of a weeklong workshop programme on fieldwork strategies. It was intended to then explore their value in the development of a field research project by a co-ordinated but still low cost survey over a specific rural area. This aimed to gather ethnographic information on village clusters and their historical trajectories in the region and relate it to local art traditions in various mediums. One of the purposes of the programme was to explore the challenges of "doing ethnography at home" from the ethnographers perspective and then evaluate ways in which they might be further enabled in a review at the end of the workshop. One key focus was to investigate the expectations and demands placed on museum researchers by local communities where the pressures for an immediate return on information are at their most intense, particularly on individuals perceived as locals. The workshop was to have considered the various strategies for establishing and maintaining dialogues with village communities and the various problems and constraints that would need to be addressed in carrying out research through the practical experiences of these ethnographers. Moreover these problems and challenges were to be shared with lower tier staff who were to be asked to contribute their experience and local knowledge to the challenges posed by this research (especially in local contacts with these communities). The long-term agenda was to provide a pilot study of how this research could be developed and carried out on a larger scale to enhance dialogue and co-operation with Western partners. At the same time it would allow an evaluation of how such partnership projects might assist in the strengthening of relations between the museum and other communities who have a stake in the making of local cultural heritage.

This project had elicited interest from a British institution but the project proposal also coincided with a wave of justifiable publicity about the trade in illicit artefacts, culminating in the spectacular discovery that the Queen was presented with a Benin bronze head in 1973 by General Gowon during a state visit. This was not as previously believed a copy but a pre-1897 Benin bronze removed from the National Museum at Lagos (Art Newspaper 2002) and contravened Nigeria's own export regulations regarding artefacts classified as antiquities. The proposed project was turned down. However it is at times such as these when such institutions are viewed with caution, if not suspicion, that they perhaps have greatest need of support and dialogue in order to assist in addressing and remedying infra-structural weaknesses. The option of avoidance by Western museums at these times is the easier less problematic choice but also one that leaves the status quo unchanged. It is a policy that ignores the harsh realities generated by weakened museum institutions in Africa. The result is that mass excavation of artefacts and the destruction of their archaeological record continue unabated. It is only through long term international co-operation and dialogue that these tragedies can perhaps be slowly stemmed through incremental change and a renewed emphasis on the multiple values of cultural heritage and the local institutions that underpin them, not through economic domination or avoidance by the West.

References

Akinola, G. (1976). 'The Origin of the Ewka Dynasty: A Study in the Use and Abuse of Oral Traditions' *Journal of the Historical Society of Nigeria* 8/3: 141-163.

Ardouin, C. (1995). 'Basic Infrastructure Problems in Local Museums'. In *Museums and the Community in West Africa* (Ardouin, C. and E. Arinze eds.), London: West African Museums Programme and the International African Institute; James Currey, pp. 45-9.

Ardouin, C. and E. Arinze (eds.) (1995) *Museums and the Community in West Africa*. London: West African Museums Programme and the International African Institute; James Currey.

Ardouin, C. and E. Arinze (eds.) (2000). *Museums and History in West Africa*. London: West African Museums Programme and the International African Institute; James Currey.

Arinze, E. (1995). 'The Training of Local Museum Staff'. In *Museums and the Community in West Africa* (Ardouin, C. and E. Arinze eds.), London: West African Museums Programme and the International African Institute; James Currey, pp. 35-44.

The Art Newspaper (2002). 'How the Queen Came to Own a Lagos Museum Piece: The Nigerian Head of State Raided a Museum to Present her with a Benin Bronze in 1973', no.128, September: 3.

Clifford, J. (1988). *The Predicament of Culture: Twentieth Century Ethnography, Literature and Art*. Cambridge. Mass.: Harvard University Press.

Coombes, A. (1994). *Reinventing Africa: Museums, Material Culture and Popular Imagination in Late Victorian and Edwardian England*. New Haven and London: Yale University Press.

Corbey, R. (2000). 'Arts Premiers in the Louvre' *Anthropology Today* 16/4: 3-6.

Gore, C. and D. Pratten (2003). 'The Politics of Plunder: The Rhetorics of Order and Disorder in Southern Nigeria' *African Affairs* 102/407 (April): 211-240.

Hannerz, U. (1989). 'Notes on the Global Ecuneme' *Public Culture* 1/2: 66-75.

Harvey, D. (1989). *The Condition of Postmodernity*. Oxford: Blackwell.

Konare, A. (1995). 'The Creation and Survival of Local Museums'. In *Museums and the Community in West Africa* (Ardouin, C. and E. Arinze eds.), London: West African Museums Programme and the International African Institute; James Currey, pp. 5-10.

O'Keefe P. (2000). *Commentary on the UNESCO 1970 Convention on Illicit Traffic*. Leicester: Institute of Art and Law, Bank Chambers. Leicester.

McIntosh, R. (1996). 'Just Say Shame: Excising the Rot of Cultural Genocide' in *Plundering Africa's Past* (Schmidt, P. and R. McIntosh eds.), London: James Currey, pp.45-62.

Picton, J. (1997). 'Edo Art, Dynastic Myth and Intellectual Aporia' *African Arts* 30/4: 18-25.

Posnansky, M. (1996). 'Coping with Collapse in the 1990s: West African Museums, Universities and National Patrimonies'. In *Plundering Africa's Past* (Schmidt, P. and R. McIntosh eds.), London: James Currey, pp. 143-163.

Prott, L. (1996). 'Saving the Heritage: UNESCO's Action against the Illicit Trade in African Antiquities'. In *Plundering Africa's Past* (Schmidt, P. and R. McIntosh eds.), London: James Currey, pp. 29-44.

Schmidt, P. and R. McIntosh (1996). 'Preface'. In *Plundering Africa's Past* (Schmidt, P. and R. McIntosh eds.), London: James Currey, pp. xi-xiii.

Shelton, A., n.d. *Cultural Property and the Reinvention of Museums: The Case of the Horniman Museum's Benin Project*. Unpublished manuscript.

Web source: http://www2.hu-berlin.de/orient/nae/ National Archives of Nigeria, Enugu Branch: Guides, Indices and Finding Aids, compiled by U.O.A. Esse, accessed 10/12/02.

4. AN OUTSIDER LOOKING IN: OBSERVATIONS ON THE AFRICAN 'ART' MARKET

Neil BRODIE

In this short contribution I can do little more than offer an outsider's perspective on the Western fetish for 'tribal art' and the damage that it is causing to African cultural heritage. A more substantial review would be book length, and indeed several books have already been written on the subject, including Steiner's (1994) *African Art in Transit* and Christiana Panella's (2002) *Les Terres Cuites de la Discorde*, and the edited volume *Plundering Africa's Past* (Schmidt and McIntosh eds. 1996). Raymond Corbey's *Tribal Art Traffic* (2000) also includes much that is relevant, and important insights into the Western reception of African heritage are offered in Sally Price's (2001) *Primitive Art in Civilized Places*. These books, taken together with the campaigning efforts of journalists such as Michel Brent (1994; 1996) and Jos van Beurden (2001a; 2001b), now constitute a solid evidence of the baleful effects that the commercial market exerts on African heritage, what Gill and Chippindale (1993) would call the intellectual and material consequences of esteem for 'African art'. Not least, perhaps, of these consequences has been the submergence of African histories and identities within a romanticised vision of Africa, in which the anonymous creativity of African tradition stands opposed to the individual authorship of the West.

The plundering of Africa's past is intimately related to the demand of Western museums and collectors for African heritage, and, latterly, the development of a commercial market. 'Ethnographic' or 'anthropological' material from Africa was first collected during the nineteenth and early twentieth centuries as part of the European imperial project, but it was not until the 1920s and 1930s that a viable commercial market became established as the aesthetic merit of some African material was 'discovered' by Western artists and connoisseurs, and awarded a price. However, by the 1950s, the supply of what Steiner calls the 'classic genres' of wooden face masks and ritual statuary had begun to dry up and the trade expanded to include household or other utilitarian objects. It also triggered a search for archaeological – in the sense of buried – objects. Most notably in West Africa the large scale and illegal excavation of terracotta statuary has been noted in the last thirty or so years.

The gradual rediscovery and removal of a West African terracotta figurative tradition can easily be followed in general syntheses of African art. For example, in the 1960 volume *Africa: the Art of the Negro Peoples*, by Elsy Leuzinger, terracottas are hardly mentioned. Indeed, Leuzinger notes that 'African clay sculptures are very delicate, and are rarely to be found in museums – and then usually in fragments' (Leuzinger 1960: 40). The book does however include a brief discussion of Nok statuary, based largely on the work of Bernard Fagg. However, by 1984, things had moved on. In Werner Gillon's *A Short History of African Art*, which was published that year, there are extended sections on Djenné and Nok terracottas. Six Djenné pieces are illustrated, two from Western museums and four from private collections. Nine Nok pieces are illustrated, seven from Nigerian museums and two from Western Museums. Gillon tells us that the first Djenné terracotta was found in 1940. In 1970 it was exhibited in the Zurich Kunsthaus, and after that date a considerable number were discovered as 'surface finds in the mud of the Inland Niger Delta' (Gillon 1984: 91). In reality, Djenné figures had been known from at least the late nineteenth century (McIntosh 1996: 53; Panella 2002: 140–54), and probably earlier, and by the late 1960s could be bought quite cheaply in Europe, although it may be true that the Zurich exhibition sparked off a collecting frenzy as prices underwent a sharp escalation after 1973 (McIntosh 1996: 47; Panella 2002: 157). In parentheses, it is interesting to note that the two promotional quotations on the back cover of the Gillon book were taken from Antiques Dealer and World of Interiors, which may perhaps indicate the books intended readership.

Gillon did not include any discussion of Bura statuettes from Niger, as these were only discovered in 1983 during excavations carried out by that country's *Institut de Recherches en Sciences Humaines* (IRSH). They were featured in an international exhibition Vallées du Niger which toured West Africa and France from 1993 to 1998, and once this exhibition had brought them to the attention of Western collectors the large scale looting of sites in Niger followed (Gado 2001: 58). Soon Bura statuettes were on sale in the West. In 2000, for example, the Hamill Gallery of African Art in Boston held an exhibition and sale entitled 'Africa Unearthed' (see http://www.hamillgallery.com/). This sale included 44 Nok pieces, predominantly heads, 4 Katsina terracottas, 6 Sokoto terracottas, 46 Bura terracotta heads, and 14 Djenné pots. Interestingly, the Djenné pieces were not for sale:

"NOT FOR SALE, although we are not personally opposed to the sale of unearthed African terracottas, we are complying with the U.S./Mali 1997 Agreement prohibiting their importation" (http://www.hamillgallery.com/).

Outrageous as it seems, it can only be assumed from this unashamed statement that the gallery's owner, Tim Hamill, is not concerned about the lost contexts of the material he sells. Indeed, as the 2002 trial of Frederick Schultz – ultimately convicted for handling antiquities illegally moved out of Egypt – shows, it is a point of view shared by most of the US trade fraternity (Gerstenblith 2002: 29). As part of a 'statement on African Art', Hamill explains why:

"I personally collect African Art because of its power, beauty, magic and craftsmanship. My viewpoint is as an artist, not as an anthropologist. I choose pieces based on formal visual criteria, some knowledge of the tribal traditions, how well I feel the piece succeeds in what it attempts and whether the work gives me an inner sense of satisfaction, pleasure and mystery. It is certainly not necessary to fully understand African art to enjoy it with a sense of wonder and awe". (http://www.hamillgallery.com/)

It is true that we are largely ignorant of the function of terracotta statuary (although see the interesting discussion in McIntosh 1996: 48–9), and we will stay that way while they are unearthed with no record and sold as art. Yet, in answer to Hamill, we can legitimately ask that if African art is not fully understood, how can the damage caused by its illicit removal be properly assessed, and dismissed?

Many of the Hammill Nok terracottas are offered with a thermoluminescence date from the Bortolot Daybreak Corporation. Bortolot's website makes for interesting reading (http://www.daybreaknuclear.com/bortolot_daybreak_frameset.html). It claims that before 1993 most Nok terracottas appearing on the market were fake, and that genuine objects were usually poorly-preserved fragments. Then, in 1993, a consortium of European dealers organized systematic looting of the Nok area, whereupon there was a flood of genuine heads and the fakes all but disappeared. Darling (2000: 17) corroborates the Bortolot story when he reports that large scale looting commenced in the Nok area in mid-1994. By 1995 two main local traders had emerged, each able to employ about 1000 diggers (*ibid*: 18). The price of Nok figures plummeted accordingly (*ibid*: 15). In 1996 visits to a small number of Parisian dealers revealed more than 50 Nok objects for sale (Shyllon 2003: 142).

We must not forget, however, that outside West Africa many different types of archaeological site are being plundered. They range from neolithic rock art sites of the Sahara (Coulson 1999; Keenan 2000) to historical shipwrecks (Abungu 2001: 45; Almeida and Lima 1995). Nor is the continent's rich Christian and Islamic heritage safe; the Christian church treasuries of Ethiopia continue to be targeted (Begashaw 1995; Van Beurden 2001b), and Islamic documents and decorative elements are also in demand (ICOM 1997: 77–9; 113–6). On the ground, local people are still forced by poverty to sell heritage, and governments have more pressing priorities than its protection. The depredations of the market are made easier by the wars that continue to afflict many African countries. Writing this in summer 2003 in the aftermath of the highly-publicised attack on Baghdad Museum I have found it difficult to obtain much news of Somalia's national museums which were ransacked when fighting broke out there in 1991 (Brandt and Mohamed 1996). Most material has now left the country but by all accounts it is still possible to buy the odd object in Mogadishu's Bakara market. Yet the press has remained remarkably quiet about the fate of Somali museums.

In 1994 the International Council of Museums (ICOM) released Looting in Africa, a volume in its 'One Hundred Missing Objects' series. It listed and illustrated objects or categories of objects that were known to have been stolen or in danger of illegal removal from museums or archaeological sites throughout Africa. By August 2003 several objects had been recovered from the possession of European dealers and collectors. No doubt more will follow (see ICOM 1997: III–IV for details). However, by the end of the 1990s the threats posed to the archaeology of West Africa were so serious that ICOM felt constrained to publish a 'Red List' of African antiquities under imminent threat of looting or theft. The list was drawn up at the AFRICOM-sponsored Workshop on the Protection of the African Cultural Heritage held in Amsterdam in October 1997 and released in May 2000. It contains eight categories of material:

- Nok terracottas from the Bauchi Plateau and the Katsina and Sokoto regions (Nigeria)
- Terracottas and bronzes from Ife (Nigeria)
- Esie stone statues (Nigeria)
- Terracottas, bronzes and pottery from the Niger Valley (Mali)
- Terracotta statuettes, bronzes, pottery, and stone statues from the Bura System (Niger, Burkina Faso)
- Stone statues from the north of Burkina Faso and neighbouring regions
- Terracottas from the north of Ghana (Komaland) and Côte d'Ivoire
- Terracottas and bronzes, so-called Sao (Cameroon, Chad, Nigeria)

It is depressing to find that a mere 17 years after their first discovery, the Bura statuettes had found their way onto the Red List of endangered objects. The Red List notes that: "These objects are among the cultural goods most affected by looting and theft. They are protected by national legislation, banned from export, and may under no circumstances be put on sale. An appeal is therefore being made to museums, action houses, art dealers and collectors to stop buying them".

Many museums around the world already refuse to acquire such objects, but sometimes the appeal falls on deaf ears. For example, the Musée Barbier-Mueller in Geneva houses a large collection of African objects (including one identified by ICOM as stolen (ICOM 1997: IV)), and in 2002, its director, Jean Paul Barbier, offered a chilling rationale for indiscriminate collecting. In a short piece headed 'On war and scruples' (Barbier 2002: 316–7), and illustrated with an image that superimposed a Bamiyan Buddha upon one of the collapsing towers of the New York World Trade Centre, he warns of the plight of terracotta statues in the northern states of Nigeria that practice Islamic Sharia law. The terracottas, according to Barbier, face reduction to dust, and he hopes that as many as possible "find shelter in Western Europe, in the New World, and in Japan." (Barbier 2002: 317). We might question Barbier's choice of Western Europe as a safe haven when we remember that during World War II something like 70,000 objects were lost from the Hamburg Museum für Völkerkunde, while at the Leipzig Museum für Völkerkunde 30,000 were destroyed in one day during an aerial bombardment (Corbey 2000: 49), although, as we have seen, historical sensibility is not a faculty that is well-developed in the hardened 'tribal art' collector. But what of the alarmist vision of extremist clerics which Barbier conjures up to frighten his readers, said to be responsible for the destruction of Christian churches and the kidnapping of European tourists, and set on the destruction of the idolatrous terracottas? The truth is that the local Muslim communities are quick to recognise a business opportunity and are happy to dig up and sell pre-Islamic artefacts (Darling 2000: 18). They are not likely to spend time and energy digging up objects only to destroy them. (Barbier omits to mention the underground provenance of these pieces, not wanting perhaps to dispel the illusion of the 'surface find' that comforts his patrons and visitors). And we should not forget the past role played by the Christian Church in destroying cultural objects for similar reasons of idolatry (Jegede 1996: 133).

In 1997 Barbier sold 276 Nigerian objects to the French Musée National des Arts d'Afrique et d'Océanie for something like 40 million French francs (Corbey 2000: 128). In 2004, this museum, together with the Musée de l'Homme, is due to be incorporated into a new and prestigious Musée des Arts et des Civilisations (officially known as the Musée du Quai Branly), a project conceived by collector and dealer Jacques Kerchache, and carried through with the support of French President Jacques Chirac. As a foretaste of what is to come, on 13th April 2000 the Louvre opened a new Pavilion des Sessions of 'tribal art' to display objects destined to be incorporated into the new museum. The Louvre display consisted of 117 artefacts including two Nok terracottas, bought from a Belgian dealer for a price claimed to be 2.5 million French francs, and a Sokoto piece. (Bailey 2000: 1). The Louvre, and Chirac, were immediately criticised for the appearance of these terracottas, not least by ICOM and the Nigerian embassy. However, in 2002, the governments of France and Nigeria reached agreement whereby France recognises that the three statues are the property of Nigeria, while Nigeria agrees for them to be retained by France on loan for a period of 25 years, on a renewable basis. Again, this agreement has been criticised as dishonourable, an outcome of French chauvinism and a neo-colonial mentality (Shyllon 2003).

Closer to home, the Royal Academy of Arts in London came under attack in 1995 when it organised an exhibition 'Africa: The Art of a Continent'. The exhibition catalogue illustrates nine Djenné terracotta figures (seven from private collections and two from Western Museums) and ten Nok figures (three from Nigerian museums and seven from private collections). The destructive origins of this material were not ignored, however, and in the section on Nok terracottas, AF spoke of "an archaeological catastrophe" (Phillips 1995: 525) and for their Djenné cousins TFG drew attention to the "Hundreds, probably thousands, of ancient sites ... ransacked and severely damaged" (Phillips 1995: 488). The Royal Academy's decision to display these pieces was met by widespread protest and a threat by the British Museum to withhold its own proposed loans if the Academy went ahead (Shaw and MacDonald 1995; Sweetman 1995). In the event, the Djenné pieces were withdrawn from the exhibition. However, in the catalogue's introduction, the editor Tom Phillips was unrepentant. While lamenting the destruction caused by the commercially motivated looting, he went on to state that it was the Royal Academy's conviction that "in the long term to show such works in this present context would not only enhance the artistic reputation of countries like Mali and Nigeria, but provoke public interest in the furtherance of archaeological activity in Africa, even to the point of attracting enabling funds" (Phillips 1995: 16–17). The exhibition was held at the Royal Academy of Arts from 4 October 1995 to 21 January 1996, nearly ten years ago, and time enough at least to allow the mobilisation of enabling funds. There is little to suggest that this has happened though.

And this is, perhaps, the crux. From the vantage point of a British university desk it is all too easy to point an accusing finger at the art market, or to ask governments and international organisations to supply political answers to African poverty and under-development, but part of the problem is simply that very few Western archaeologists work in Africa, and thus very little Western research funding finds its way there. Part of the answer to the problems posed to Africa by the art market is simply that more archaeological research should take place there.

References

Abungu, G. (2001). 'Examples from Kenya and Somalia'. In *Trade in Illicit Antiquities: the Destruction of the World's Archaeological Heritage* (Brodie, N., J. Doole and C. Renfrew eds.), Cambridge: McDonald Institute, pp. 37-46.

Almeida, J. and A. Lima (1995). 'The situation in the Cape Verde Islands with reference to illicit traffic: problems and proposals'. In *ICOM 1995: Illicit Traffic of Cultural Property in Africa*, Paris: ICOM, pp. 41-6.

Bailey, M. (2000). 'Chirac intervenes in illicit art trade' *Art Newspaper* (June) no. 104: 1-9.

Barbier, J. (2002). 'Confidentially yours' *Arts and Cultures* No. 3 (1977–2002: 25th Anniversary of the Barbier-Mueller Museum): 297–318.

Begashaw, K. (1995). 'Illicit traffic of cultural heritage in north-east Africa'. In *ICOM 1995: Illicit Traffic of Cultural Property in Africa*, Paris: ICOM, pp. 55-62.

Brandt, S. and O. Mohamed (1996). 'Starting from scratch: the past, present and future management of Somalia's cultural heritage'. In *Plundering Africa's Past* (Schmidt, P. and R. McIntosh eds.), London: James Currey, pp. 250–60.

Brent, M. (1994). 'The rape of Mali' *Archaeology* 47/3: 26–35

Brent, M. (1996). 'A view inside the illicit trade in African antiquities'. In *Plundering Africa's Past* (Schmidt, P. and R.J. McIntosh eds.), London: James Currey, pp. 63-78.

Corbey, R. (2000). *Tribal Art Traffic*. Amsterdam: Royal Tropical Institute.

Coulson, D. (1999). 'Saharan rock art' *National Geographic* 195/6: 104–19.

Darling, P. (2000). 'The rape of Nok and Kwatakwashi: the crisis in Nigerian antiquities' *Culture Without Context* 6: 15–20.

Gado, B. (2001). 'The Republic of Niger'. In *Trade in Illicit Antiquities: the Destruction of the World's Archaeological Heritage* (Brodie, N., J. Doole and C. Renfrew eds.), Cambridge: McDonald Institute, pp. 57–72.

Gill, D. and C. Chippindale (1993). 'Material and intellectual consequences of esteem for Cycladic figures' *American Journal of Archaeology* 97: 601–59.

Gillon, W. (1984). *A Short History of African Art*. New York: Viking.

Gerstenblith, P. (2002). 'United States v. Schultz' *Culture Without Context* 10: 27–31.

ICOM (1997). *Looting in Africa*. Paris: ICOM.

Jegede, D. (1996). 'Nigerian art as endangered species'. In *Plundering Africa's Past* (Schmidt, P. and R. McIntosh eds.), London: James Currey, pp. 125–42.

Keenan, J. (2000). 'The theft of Saharan rock-art' *Antiquity* 74: 287–8.

Leuzinger, E. (1960). *Africa: the Art of the Negro Peoples*. London: Methuen.

McIntosh, R. (1996). 'Just say shame: excising the rot of cultural genocide'. In *Plundering Africa's Past* (Schmidt, P. and R. McIntosh eds.), London: James Currey, pp. 45–62.

Panella, C. (2002). *Les Terres Cuites de la Discorde*. Leiden: Research School CNWS, publications no. 113).

Phillips, T. (1995). *Africa: the Art of a Continent*. London: Royal Academy of Arts.

Price, S. (2001). *Primitive Art in Civilized Places*. Chicago: University of Chicago Press.

Schmidt, P. and R. McIntosh (eds.) (1996). *Plundering Africa's Past*. London: James Currey.

Shaw, T. and K. MacDonald (1995). 'Out of Africa and out of context' *Antiquity* 69: 1036–9.

Shyllon, F. (2003). 'Negotiations for the return of Nok sculptures from France to Nigeria – an unrighteous conclusion' *Art, Antiquity and Law* 8: 133–48.

Steiner, C. (1994). *African Art in Transit*. Cambridge: Cambridge University Press.

Sweetman, D. (1995). 'The Government, the terracotta, and the Academy' *Independent Newspaper* (Section Two) 26th September.

Van Beurden, J. (2001a). *Goden, Graven en Grenzen: Over Kunstroof uit Afrika, Azië en Latijns-Amerika*. Amsterdam: KIT.

Van Beurden, J. (2001b). 'A holy cross and the necessity for international conventions' *Culture Without Context* 9: 30–1.

5. CONSERVATION OF ROCK ART IN THE SAHARA

Alberto LAROCCA

INTRODUCTION

The archaeological, anthropological and artistic value of Saharan rock art is immense. This art, produced in prehistoric and proto-historic times (from about the fourth millennium BC onwards) is perhaps the most remarkable legacy of the populations that inhabited the once lush Sahara. Although after World War Two the rock art sites attracted the attention of many researchers -- particularly French and Italian (e.g. Lhote 1976; Mori 1965) -- the subject does not receive the attention it deserves, and this is mainly due to the historical and political circumstances of the region. In fact, the rock art is found mainly in the Central Saharan massifs of Algeria, Libya, Mali, Niger, Chad, Morocco, and to a lesser extent in Mauritania and Egypt (Muzzolini 1995: 9-26; fig. 5.1). Most of these countries are experiencing, or have experienced, serious political and economical problems: economic stagnation, civil wars, rebellions and border disputes are a common feature. For example, Libya was isolated from the international community by an embargo that lasted for nearly a decade and that was lifted only months ago. Libya was also at war (from 1972 to 1994) with Chad over the control of the northern Tibesti, a region rich in uranium; Algeria is torn by civil war, which has caused more than 100,000 deaths; Morocco, Mauritania and Algeria were engaged in a conflict over the possession of Western Sahara and the Malian government has no power in its Saharan provinces, which are controlled by the Tuareg. A similar situation is experienced in northern Chad, where bandits defeated the governmental army and now rule the area. The political instability adds to the economic struggles of these countries, which are affected by seemingly unstoppable desertification, very high unemployment and the disinterest of foreign investors and aid agencies. The combination of these factors meant that the conservation of the natural and historical heritage was most often given the lowest priority. Not only has archaeological research slowed down considerably, but also existing conservation projects were suspended owing to lack of funding. Therefore the local authorities in these countries do not have the financial means to manage archaeological sites, which are regularly looted and damaged. However, as a rule, the authorities are now designing and implementing plans to help preserve cultural heritage, through the creation of protected areas and the development of sustainable forms of eco-tourism involving the local communities. At the base of a successful conservation strategy there must be a realistic assessment of the situation, which takes into account not only the technical problems related to the conservation of the rock art, but also the role of the local community and the social impact of any proposed plan of action. The first step is the identification of the problems, and then a conservation plan must be designed by the authorities working with technicians and the local community.

THE PROBLEMS

The volatile political situation of many Saharan countries forced archaeologists, both local and foreign, to cease most of the research projects in the region. Therefore it is difficult to assess with certainty the nature and the extent of the damage to rock art, particularly in countries such as Niger, Mali and Chad, where social unrest is more acute. For example the Adrar des Iforas in the Malian Sahara is only accessible with a military escort, and even then the risk of being ambushed by rebels is extremely high. As a consequence, there are no reports on the state of conservation of the archaeological sites in the Adrar des Iforas, as confirmed recently by a Malian official. The only positive side of this isolation is that damage by to tourists is minimised. In fact, the isolation experienced in the mid 1990s in southern Algeria allowed a relatively good conservation assessment of the rock art sites in the Tassili n-Ajjer and the Hoggar. It is only since the return to a more fragile stability that damage to archaeological sites has occurred, in concomitance with an increase in tourism.

The natural factors that most affect the conservation of Saharan rock art are linked to the nature of the rock surface and the climate. Rock art is always found in open air, exposed sites and mainly on sandstone, which under the extreme weather conditions of the region is very friable. The exfoliation of the rock surface is particularly rapid when directly exposed to the elements, without any shelter or overhang. Furthermore, the action of rain (although not frequent in the Sahara) has devastating effects, dissolving the salt in the rock and bringing it to the surface, thus accelerating the foliation process. Although the action of the climate has profound effects on the rock art, the major threats come from human action, and both local communities and foreigners are to blame. Even though at present we do not have reports on the state of rock art sites in the Saharan regions, we can assume that the damages to the rock art observed in Libya, Morocco and Algeria represent a sample that can be extended to the rest of the Saharan nations. I will analyse the cases of these three countries, highlighting particularly problems that may be

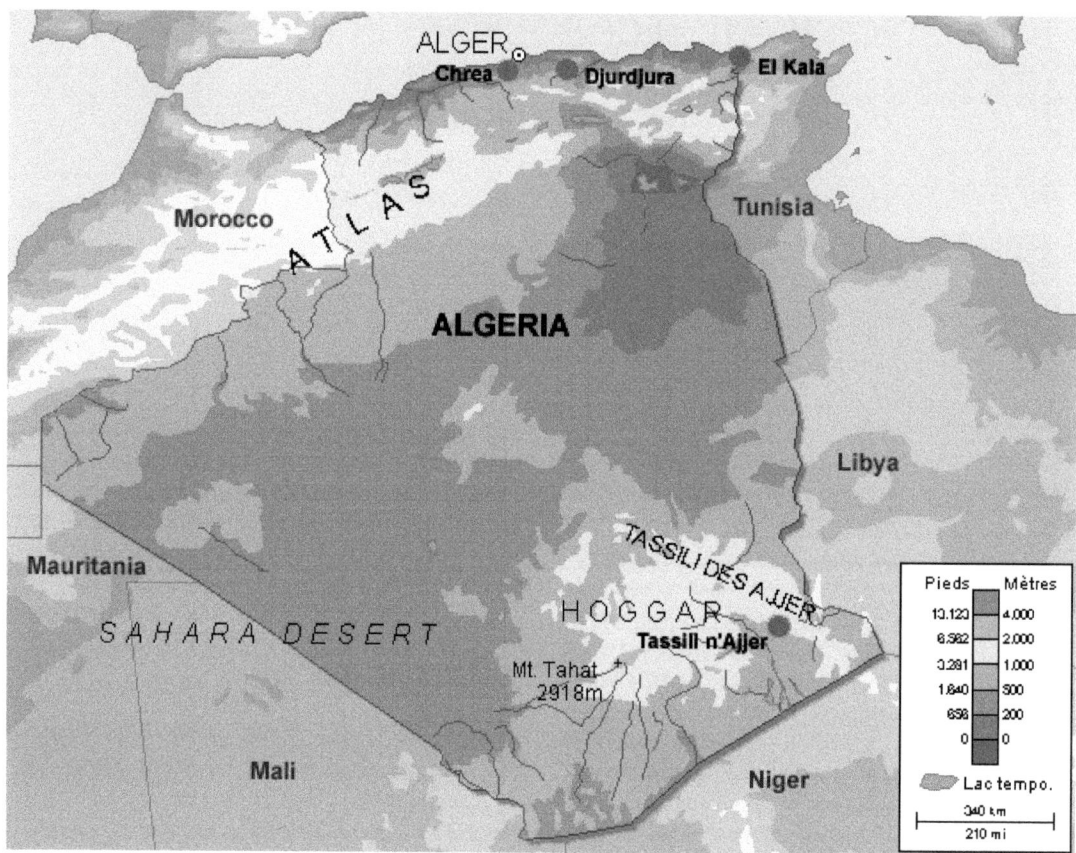

Fig. 5.1 Map showing general area under consideration

ascribed to tourism, mineral exploitation and after inadequate conservation policies.

MOROCCO

Morocco has always been the Northern African country most open to the West. As a consequence, both public and private investors have injected large sums to boost the national economy, especially its tourism industry. However, Morocco's historic sites have often suffered from a non-regulated influx of tourists, which could not be supported by an adequate infrastructure. The large number of visitors accelerated the deterioration of several rock art sites, and the lack of control allowed unscrupulous tourists and art dealers or collectors to loot many sites. In a recent trip to the Jebel Bani region in the south of Morocco, I witnessed some very alarming cases of mismanagement, all ascribable directly to financial underfunding from Government sources. The site of Imaoun, recently studied by Susan Searight (Searight 1996), is extraordinarily rich in rock art and is being plundered by local people who sell pieces of painted rock as souvenirs. Tourists and collectors also cut the engravings from the rock with hammer and chisel. According to local guides the same practice is widespread in the rest of the rock art sites in the south of Morocco. The pillage is facilitated by the scarcity of wardens, who are not able to cover efficiently such a vast area. Furthermore, several sites are within easy reach from the main tarmac road, and are sometimes even indicated by large signposts, as in the case of the sites of the Adrar Metgourine. Here, there are some of the most interesting rock art sites of this part of the Sahara in terms of density and variety of styles and motifs (Rodrigue 1993). The lithic industry of the Adrar Metgourine is also very rich, showing that the area was inhabited since the Mousterian (Rodrigue 1987). Despite the wealth of its archaeological material, the Adrar is not protected yet although the site is clearly indicated (in French only) by signposts along the main road. Needless to say that this area has also experienced extensive plundering by locals who use decorated stone boulders as a construction material to build new houses in the nearby oasis town of Akka and who also sell this material on to collectors and dealers. It appears to me that in the near future the situation is not going to ameliorate; at present, the sites are 12 kilometres off the tarmac road, and the state of the track is, in parts, poor. However the locals suggest that there are rumours of a plan to build a tarmac road to link the main road to a nearby village via the Adrar Metgourine, which would eventually lead to the site of Imaoun. Of course, if access to the sites (even for locals) is not somehow regulated, the looting and the deterioration of the rock art will inevitably increase: another cause of deterioration of rock art sites are the fires lit by shepherds in shelters which deposit a film of soot on the rock surface (Alaoui and Searight 1997; TARA 1998).

ALGERIA

Owing to the volatile political situation and the consequent political isolation of the country, Algeria has not suffered as much as Morocco from of the influx of foreign tourists. The most serious threat to Algerian rock art comes from thieves that exploit the absence of governmental management control. Jeremy Keenan has reported how hundreds of paintings and engravings were chiselled off the rock in the Tassilli n-Ajjer (on the World Heritage List) and in the Hoggar (Keenan 2000). There is reason to believe that this is the action not only of tourists (the few that actually cross the border with Libya with 4x4 vehicles) in search of souvenirs, but also of professional thieves who loot archaeological sites and sell the artefacts to private collectors on the European and American markets. These looters sometimes succeed in steeling the art intact, but most often the rock is too fragile and crumbles during extraction (Keenan 2000). The thieves can act freely, since there is little control along the borders. Furthermore the local authorities do not have enough staff of the financial means to assume an efficient policing role. The theft is not limited to the parietal rock art; portable art such as figurines, decorated objects and ostrich eggshells and stone tools, which can still be found in considerable quantities in the remotest areas of the Sahara, are all regularly stolen.

The people inhabiting these regions have little interest in the rock art, which they do not consider to be part of their cultural heritage (Jeremy Keenan pers. comm.); children often play in the decorated rock shelters, writing on the walls and generally vandalising the sites; also adults show little respect for the rock art. In the Tassilli n-Ajjer (Algeria) and in the Fezzan-Acacus (Libya) bullet holes on paintings and engravings have also been observed (TARA 1998; Keenan pers. comm.). It appears that the art has been used for target practice by bandits operating in the central Saharan region. Furthermore Muslim fundamentalist groups have intentionally destroyed some paintings (this is in accordance with fundamentalist Islamic concepts of human representation). Sadly some archaeologists, while experimenting with new conservation techniques have not helped; one of the most famous panels in the Sahara, the painting of the 'Great God of Sefar' was chosen by a team of archaeologists to experiment a resin that should have created a protective polymeric film over the painted rock surface. The result was catastrophic: two areas of the panel were irreparably damaged. This added to the deterioration caused by other common archaeological practices, such as wetting the rock surface to enhance the colours prior to recording (see TARA 1998).

LIBYA

The two major causes of concern for the preservation of archaeological sites in Libya are the damage caused by unregulated tourism, and the action of oil companies. The political isolation generated by the recent embargo on the country pushed the Libyan government into adopting a 'soft' policy towards tourists, who could insure the entry of hard currency, especially in the desert areas of the south which became the target for unregulated tourism. The archaeological sites of the Akakus are particularly affected by the uncontrolled influx of tourists, mainly from Italy, Germany and France. According some to recent estimates, 45,000 people visited the region from December 1999 and April 2000, thanks also to the fully operational airport of Ghat (S. Di Lernia pers. comm.) Some European tour operators are now promoting the rock art sites of the Akakus as a major attraction, and have even set up vast tented camps which can accommodate up to 600 people right at the foot of decorated rock shelters. Of course the easy access to the area and the little care paid by both local people and tourists has accelerated the deterioration of the natural landscape and the archaeological sites of the area. The current situation is depressing: in a recent survey, 40 sites have been reported to be seriously damaged by irresponsible behaviour and looting (S. Di Lernia pers. comm.). There is the habit among tourists of wetting with water or oil the rock surface in order to enhance the colours of the paintings and take better pictures, which accelerates the exfoliation process and destroys the pigments. Unfortunately, the guides do nothing to stop these practices; on the contrary, it has been brought to my attention that they sometimes steal artefacts and sell them as souvenirs. The excessive influx of people in the area also has an environmental upon fauna and vegetation in these fragile ecozones.

Another cause of damage to Saharan rock art sites is the action of oil companies that operate in the Sahara. Often the need for infrastructural and economic development overrides the necessity for conservation of natural and cultural heritage. Companies that utilise heavy equipment for geological surveys damage the rock surface simply by the vibrations created by the vehicles, let alone when they are performing major works, such as drilling or the construction of roads. The oil company LASMO in particular has been accused of disfiguring the landscape and damaging archaeological sites in the Messak, where they discovered a very rich oil field (Le Quellec 2001). LASMO admitted that the surveys carried out in the Messak might have caused some damage, so they sponsored two teams, one Italian and one British, in order to assess the causes and extent of the damage. The results are now widely debated; the report (Cremaschi *et al.* 2000) was judged to be too indulgent towards LASMO, not stressing enough the seriousness of the deterioration of the archaeological sites. In the same issue of *Sahara* D. Coulson -- also invited by LASMO to give an assessment of the situation -- described the damage to both landscape and rock art, and proposed a number of actions that LASMO should take towards a correct exploitation of the territory (Coulson 2000). In May 2001, in occasion of the annual meeting of the *Association des Amis de l'Art Rupestre Saharienne*, Le Quellec offered a more pessimistic view of the situation in the Messak, highlighting how LASMO made little effort to respect the natural and cultural heritage of the region and the impressive extent and gravity of the damage (Le Quellec 2001). It seems that different researchers give different assessments of the same situation; neither can agree as to the seriousness of the problem and without such an academic consensus meaningful and effective action is unlikely.

The archaeologists that are in charge of the study and conservation of the rock art here have also been the cause of some damage (as in Algeria), although not maliciously rather through sheer carelessness. Some of the recording techniques utilised in the past, (such as moulding) had a physical, chemical impact on the rock surface, which resulted in crumbling of the rock face (Bednarik 1990). In the 1980s a team of Italian researchers in the Akakus made several casts of engravings and experimented with some synthetic resins for conservation measures, however this only resulted in damage to the rock art itself (Le Quellec 2001).

POSSIBLE CONSERVATION MEASURES

There are several measures that need to be taken in order to formulate an efficient conservation plan. However, the strategy cannot be decided unless a detailed assessment of the situation is undertaken. The initial inventory would aim at the detailed recording of all rock art sites and their state of conservation; this is a process requiring specialised technical expertise, time and great financial outlay. The financial situation is particularly difficult since Saharan rock art is not as popular a tourist or academic 'draw' as the rock art of, for example, Australia or France, and as a consequence archaeological research in the Sahara attracts funding with only great difficulty from the wider international community; political instability in the region does not assist matters either. In order to draw attention to the rock art and its conservation, some Saharan governments created national parks and inscribed the most endangered sites on the World Heritage List (WHL). For example, in Algeria the Tassili n-Ajjer National Park was founded in 1972 and declared a World Heritage Site in 1986. Similarly, the Tadrart-Acacus became a World Heritage Site in 1986 (MAB 1995). The aim of Algeria and Libya was to highlight the immense value of the rock art and the risks to it. With the addition of the sites to the WHL, they were also hoping to receive help in the form of financial assistance, equipment, staff and education programmes. Unfortunately, the political situation put a halt to the conservation plans, and in any case the status of World Heritage Site does not guarantee financial assistance (see also Finneran this volume).

In the Tassili n-Ajier, the inventory of the rock art is not complete yet, and new sites are being continuously discovered. In Mali, Mauritania, Chad and Niger there is very little research in progress, and it is feared that the sites may have suffered irreparable damage. In Libya and Morocco the recording programme is ongoing, and is far off completion (Cremaschi *et al.* 2000; Alaoui and Searight 1997). The inventory showed that both in the Acacus and the Saharan Atlas the rock art has been looted and extensively damaged, thus stressing the need of urgent conservation measures. It must be stressed that the survey must be conducted using low impact methods, and not using techniques (such as moulding) that would worsen the state of conservation of the rock art.

Once the inventory is complete an overall strategy for conservation can be framed. But who is to take such a decision? Governmental personnel, or members of the local community, or both? If it is true that the local communities do not seem to claim 'ancestral' rights on the rock art, certainly they are those who will be affected directly by any measure taken. There is in my view a tendency to put in charge of the management of archaeological sites experts nominated by the government, who tend to neglect the role and wishes of the local community, and there is a general lack of consultation or integration. In my opinion collaboration should always be sought, rather than direct imposition of decisions from above. Certainly, the first step is to recognise the value of the rock art sites and declare them protected areas, as was done in Algeria, Libya and Morocco. However, the effective policing of the territory would be impossible if operated only by appointed guards. For example, the Tassilli National Park covers an area of 80,000 Km^2; it is patrolled by 82 guards, i.e. each guard has to patrol nearly 1,000Km^2 (MAB 1995)! The only viable solution, therefore, is the involvement of the local community in the management of the archaeological sites; at every stage it should be emphasised, even if the modern inhabitants feel little empathy towards the rock art (as is common among Islamic communities) that its destruction would have profound implications for the local economy

The construction of physical barriers to protect the rock art from the action of the weather and humanity is not the ultimate solution. Creating artificial shelters could certainly help protecting the rock surface from the rain, but it would not stop looters or the most determined tourists. Instead, there are some precautionary measures that I believe are more important: awareness campaigns, delegation of tasks to the local community and development of eco-tourism. The artistic and archaeological value of Saharan rock art is unknown to many of the local communities. They simply do not believe that the art was done by their ancestors (and this, at least for the Neolithic rock art, is probably true). Nevertheless, even if they are not interested in the historical value of rock art, they should be made aware of the economic potential of it, especially in regions that have no other sources of income. Thus, the local authorities should inform the community of the several values of the rock art, especially the younger generations, so that the population will have a different perception of the archaeological sites. The value of rock art should be highlighted in western countries, from which most of the tourists, and collectors and dealers, come. Very often tourists do not operate maliciously. They simply do not know that their actions can have irreversible negative effects not only on the rock art, but also on the natural landscape. Certainly, the involvement of big European tour operators did not ameliorate the behaviour of the tourists to these once remote areas. On the contrary, the damage to the archaeological and natural heritage has multiplied exponentially. However, some journalists are now actively involved in the education of the European public, writing about the meanings of Saharan rock art, its conservation and the behaviour that the tourists should assume when in the desert and at archaeological sites (e.g. Semplici 1999 *passim*).

As for the management of the rock art sites, the local community should be entrusted with the greater part of the responsibility. As previously mentioned, the few resources available do not allow the efficient patrolling of the areas protected. This is clearly exemplified by the case of the Tassilli National Park, where a few guards must cover huge territories. Here, most of the staff was recruited in local villages and trained up to a high standard. A more practical way of proceeding might be the education of the whole population, rather than of a small part of it. In this way, every member of the community would be able to give a contribution in the safeguarding of the natural and cultural heritage by performing simple, but vital duties. Of course, there would still be the need for more specialised personnel, which would be trained for more 'technical' tasks.

The local community should be significantly involved in the development of a sustainable form of tourism, which would allow the economic exploitation of the rock art sites without endangering them. Clearly, the big European tour operators do not represent a solution. In fact, in this instance the money generated from the rock art is not injected back into the local community, but it enriches the European owners. Small businesses run by local people would create job opportunities and flow of capital, and it would boost the conservation efforts of the local community. Thus, the rock art would be considered as a major source of income, and not as a valuable artefact to steal and sell to western collectors and tourists. Furthermore, it has been suggested that the local tour operators and guides should be trained, enlisted and held co-responsible for the damage done by their groups to archaeological material (Cremaschi *et al.* 2000).

The development of an eco-friendly tourist industry can only be achieved if central governments and local community cooperate. This at least has been recognised by Morocco; in 1995 an international conference on mountain tourism in Marrakech brought to the attention of governments and the tourism industry the issue of rock art conservation and the increase of tourism in these areas. As a consequence, the Moroccan government has promoted the collaboration between the Antiquities Department and the communities of the High Atlas. The *Institut National des Sciences de l'Archéologie et du Patrimonie* is providing technicians for the recording of the rock art, while the local community has the duty of safeguarding the sites and controlling the influx and the activities of the tourists in the protected area (Alaoui and Searight 1997). Unfortunately, lack of funding hinders the successful application of this conservation plan.

As regards to the action of oil companies in the Sahara, this represents a very delicate issue because oil exploitation is the most lucrative business in the region. However, there are ways to find a compromise between exploitation of resources and conservation of natural and cultural heritage. For example, in the debate over LASMO in Libya, the one suggestion upon which all observers agreed is that the damage can be limited if high-tech equipment is used for exploration and exploitation of oil fields. Furthermore, an archaeological survey prior to any mining or prospecting operation is necessary in order to avoid irreversible damage to the sites that stand in the way of the development. However, the question remains: who should be in charge of the archaeological survey? Is it ethically correct that archaeologists work for those companies that most threaten the archaeological resource? How free to act can an archaeological team sponsored by a chemical company be, and could it resist the political pressure? Should a completely independent body be created and managed by UNESCO for such preliminary surveys? These are all considerations that have ramifications far beyond the Sahara region, and are central to the global debate on archaeological ethics.

CONCLUSION

It is impossible to suggest one universally applicable strategy, because each and every case is different. However, the involvement of the local community is of paramount importance for the success of a conservation plan. In the Sahara there are encouraging signs that there is the will for taking stringent measures in order to preserve an invaluable cultural heritage. In Libya, the Tadrart-Acacus National Park will soon be operating. In Algeria, the government and the local communities are willing to exploit the rock art sites responsibly and as a precious source of income. Morocco offers one of the first cases of successful cooperation between national institutions and local communities. It is hoped that also in Chad, Mali and Niger -- once the political situation has stabilised -- the conservation of the rock art will be again on the agenda of politicians. In the meantime, in Europe we have the duty to divulge the artistic and archaeological value of Saharan rock art and its state of conservation. We should also educate the public to a more responsible approach to these archaeological sites and natural landscapes that, because of our inconsiderate and careless behaviour, are now under extreme threat.

References

Alaoui, F. and S. Searight (1997). 'Rock Art in Morocco' *Proceedings of the Prehistoric Society* 63: 87-101.

Bednarik, R. (1990). 'About professional vandals' *Survey* 4/6: 8-12.

Coulson, D. (2000). 'Threats and hopes for archaeological preservation' *Sahara* 12: 179.

Cremaschi, M., S. Di Lernia and M. Liverani (2000). 'The "archaeological park" of the Tadrat Acacus and Messale Settafet (south-west Fezzan, Algeria)' *Sahara* 12: 121 - 140.

Keenan, K. (2000). 'The theft of Saharan rock-art' *Antiquity* 74: 287-8.

Le Quellec, J-L. (2001). 'Quelques images de la dégradation du Messak'. Unpublished paper presented at Pinerolo, 25th May 2001, Annual Meeting of the Association de l'Art Rupestre Saharienne.

Lhote, H. (1976). *Les Gravures Rupestres de l'Oued Djerat*. Algiers: Mémoires du C.R.A.P.E.

MAB (Man and the Biosphere Programme UNESCO) (1995). *Tassili N'Ajjer National Park. News from the MAN National Committees*. Algiers: UNESCO.

Mori, F. (1965). *Tadrart Acacus: Arte Rupestre e Culture del Sahara Preistorico*. Turin: Einaudi.

Muzzolini, A. (1995). *Les Images Rupestres du Sahara.* Toulouse: Muzzolini.

Rodrigue, A. (1987). 'Nouveaux éléments sur le Moustérien du Maroc. La station d'Akka (Maroc Saharien)' *L'Anthropologie* 91/2: 483-496.

Rodrigue, A. (1993). 'Documents rupestres de l'Adrar Metgourine (Maroc Saharien)' *Bulletin de la Société d'Études et de Recherches Préhistoriques Les Eyzies* 42: 49-61.

Searight, S. (1996). 'Imaoun: a unique rock art site in South Morocco' *Sahara* 8: 79-82.

Semplici, A. (1999). *Libia.* Turin: UTET.

TARA (Trust for African Rock Art) (1998). *TARA Newsletter* Volume 8: 2.

6. ETHICS AND THE AFRICAN ARCHAEOLOGIST: THE CASE OF MALI

Kevin MACDONALD

INTRODUCTION

Over the past decade the increasing looting and destruction of West African cultural heritage has finally begun to affect the way that regional Africanist archaeologists practice. The relevance of 'pure' research, untempered by community outreach or *sensibilisation*, is being increasingly held up to question (cf. Bedaux and Rowlands 2001). Additionally, Africanists working in European and American institutions have, with increasing vigour, worked in their own countries against unethical activities in the art world (e.g. McIntosh 1991; 1996; Inskeep 1992; Shaw and MacDonald 1995). Surely, to be an Africanist archaeologist today, one should be equally concerned with research quality and issues of cultural heritage management.

So, what then must we do? To begin, I believe that we have been far too concerned about shutting the door after the horse has bolted. International legislative efforts and policing the borders against an outflow of looted antiquities is all very well, but it will not retrieve the contexts of pillaged items. It will also not restore the portions of sites destroyed by looting activities. It will only confirm in the minds of the avaricious and uneducated the supposedly inherent value of such objects. Our task, rather, is to valorise the *context* of artefacts for learning about the past -- by getting locals on the side of researchers, and by shaming collectors to reduce the demand that drives the entire antiquities looting process. We, as Africanist archaeologists, cannot merely stand by, bewail the situation and expect the *gendarmerie* to do something for us. We must paddle our own boat, by taking action both when abroad and when at home.

ACTION IN AFRICA

Good field research goes hand-in-hand with good local understanding and the passage of some tangible benefit (beyond immediate financial gain) to local communities. One of the most complete ethical codes for the archaeologist (of which I am aware) is that of Healey (1984), published in *Ethics and Values in Archaeology*. In essence, it puts forward the following principals for comportment abroad:

1. Comply with local laws and respect the host country's archaeological regulations (especially regarding decisions for the temporary or permanent exportation of archaeological materials)

2. Collaborate effectively with host country scholars, and provide them free of charge with all publications stemming from the archaeological project.

3. Communicate with the host community via public presentations or exhibitions the results of the archaeological project (even if such presentations are local and informal)

4. Avoid 'short-termism' in research projects and assist the host country with cultural resource management via aid with site and artefact conservation.

Although all four of these major points should now be viewed as essential, we are particularly concerned here with the latter two. As Healey (1984: 129) notes regarding community work:

> "People... find it surprising to see foreigners coming to their homeland to spend large sums of money on equipment, supplies and labour just for the sake of 'research'. There is a natural tendency to be just a little suspicious that 'profit' is being made, and probably at their expense."

Therefore, local people need to be involved as more than a source of cheap labour. Both explanation, and a real exchange of perspectives is needed. This sort of community based approach has seen much success in the vicinity of Jenne-Jeno through the *sensibilisation* work of Boubacar Diaby (Head of the Mission Culturelle de Djenné), Rogier Bedaux, and the McIntoshes (Dembélé and van der Waals 1991; McIntosh *et al.* 1995; McIntosh 1996). Similarly, during the Douentza Project of 1993-96, Dr. Téréba Togola and I made local language radio broadcasts about the difference between looting and archaeological research. In our first year, with the aid of local officials, we were able to close down the business of the local *antiquaire* and subsequently, via lectures to our workers and local radio broadcasts, we have felt a heightened community involvement and support. Indeed, we have seen no new looting trenches in the Douentza area since our campaign of excavation and local *sensibilisation* began there in 1993 (MacDonald *et al.* 1994). Clearly, community involvement is worth the extra time and effort.

Site conservation is often more problematic, as it involves additional expense and expertise to which not all archaeologists will have access. Additionally, at least in West Africa, most major sites take the form of either open air settlement mounds or rockshelters. Regarding the former, Kiethega (1995: 52) notes "these mounds may be close to existing villages, but they are not spectacular and do not attract tourists. Their wealth lies in material that is buried underground." Although large scale exposures on such sites will eventually reveal the foundations of extensive building complexes, the conservation of recognisable mudbrick 'city-scapes' for local or foreign tourism remains a daunting task. In all likelihood, tells will remain for some time, potsherd littered 'debris-scapes' in need of the interpretation and protection of resident archaeologists or local guides. Their conservation even as integral mound is also not a simple matter -- *vide* recent attempts to protect Jenne-Jeno from erosion via 'green-belts' or 'termite-belts' (R.J. McIntosh pers. comm.). However, Boubacar Diaby and his *Mission Culturelle de Djenné* has gone a long way to valorise their local UNESCO World Heritage tell site of Jenné-jeno. By the education and licensing of local guides, and by exhibitions and theatre performances in local villages, *the Mission Culturelle de Djenné* has worked to both protect the Jenné area from looters and to attract tourists -- not to mention encouraging local historical pride (Bedaux and Rowlands 2001).

Rockshelters pose fewer problems, but are also less imposing than the monumental tells of Mali. A good example here is that of Korounkorokalé, 27 kilometres south of Bamako. This rockshelter, excavated in the 1950s by a colonial official and again in 1992-93 by the author (MacDonald 1997), provides the longest occupation sequence yet known from Mali (over 7000 years). Almost gutted by the original excavations, we removed half of the remaining few square metres of deposits so as to radiocarbon date its sequence, and secured the remainder. There was little left for the public to disturb. In collaboration with our team, Jon Anderson and Salif Kanouté of the *Opération Aménagement et Production Forestieres du Mali* (OAPF) assembled a narrative panel in French and Malinke outlining the occupation sequence of the shelter. Initially we took this around to local villages and made presentations with the aid of an *animateur* from the OAPF. This has now been erected at the site, along with a road marker. In this way the site becomes both a useful local focus, and a touristic diversion.

Plans are also afoot to clean up and interpret *Point G*, one of the few rock art sites in immediate proximity to the capital (D. Keita pers. comm.). Protecting such sites from vandalism, while maintaining the aesthetic appeal of their immediate environment, is an ongoing problem for rock art localities in Africa. Of course, in the case of *Point G* it would be difficult not to improve it, being situated as it is amidst one of the capitals burgeoning waste disposal areas.

Most recently, a unique international project took place in the region of Dia, in the Inland Niger Delta of Mali. Dia is situated in the middle of a heavily looted area where most sites have been pillaged for 'Jenné-style' terracotta statuettes. Due to large-scale pillaging, the number of affected sites in the region has been rapidly increasing (more than c. 80 % in 2000). The time had come to get as much data as possible from a major site in the region before it was too late. We thus decided to undertake major 'proactive salvage excavations' at Dia. To facilitate this, an international consortium was formed led by Professor Rogier Bedaux of the Museum voor Volkenkunde, Leiden; and including archaeologists from the Universities of Paris, University College London, and all Malian heritage organizations. The result was a five year field project which began in 1998, and which ultimately will culminate in a monograph and exhibitions both in Mali and Europe (cf. Bedaux *et al.* 2001).

It is important that excavations are not merely seen as a means to produce short-term research results. We should begin to build into research schedules time for local explanation, and local exhibition of findings. Optimally, as has been done at Jenné-Jeno and Korounkorokalé, we need to establish local museums or explanatory plaques to encourage appropriate cultural tourism. Local groups who value their past are less likely to let harm befall its vestiges. Would villagers at Avebury stand mutely by while someone came along with a lorry and started carting off the stones?

ACTION AT HOME

A topic not covered by Healey's ethical code, is the proper involvement of the Western archaeologist in the fight against looting at home. Over the past decade action has been taken at four levels: 1) anti-authentication efforts (via either dating or personal evaluation), 2) efforts to prohibit the public display of looted or stolen objects, 3) attempts at increasing public awareness of art market corruption, and 4) support of legislative measures to ban the import of antiquities without permit. All of these actions taken together heighten a sense of illegality associated with the antiquities trade and hopefully makes the collection of illicit items less desirable (again the 'shame' factor).

Anti-authentication efforts exemplified by the controversy which surrounded the Oxford accelerator unit in the early 1990s. At that time, thermoluminescence dates run by the Oxford University Research Laboratory for Archaeology and the History of Art, were the primary means of authentication for looted Malian terracottas. A motion of condemnation by the Society of Africanist Archaeologists in 1990 (McIntosh 1991), and a letter-writing campaign led by Ray Inskeep (1992) of Oxford and Chris Chippendale (1991), the editor of *Antiquity*, led to a change in policy at Oxford to the effect that "Dating and authentication will no longer be undertaken for private individuals or commercial salesrooms and galleries" (McIntosh 1996: 58). This is but one example of what unified action of the foreign archaeological community can accomplish.

Museum policies to prohibit the exhibition of looted objects, combined with campaigning by academic archaeologists have met with more varied levels of success. A *cause célèbre* in which I was involved was the

Africa Art of a Continent exhibition at the Royal Academy of Arts (for more detail see Shaw and MacDonald 1995). This exhibition, probably the largest exposition of African arts and antiquities yet mounted in Britain, was to feature a number of looted Jenné terracottas from the collections of private individuals. Various academics questioned the propriety of showing these pieces, and the British Museum even threatened to withhold the loan of items from its collections if these terracottas were displayed. Ultimately, the Royal Academy backed down, but still showed life-size colour transparencies of the objects, as well as nearly 400 pieces of questionable provenance from private collections. These pieces included looted terracottas from other regions of West Africa and looted metalwork from the vicinity of Jenne itself. To add insult to injury, an Igbo-Ukwu pot stolen from the reserve of the Department of Archaeology at Ibadan, though arguably recovered from dealers by the Royal Academy, was scheduled for exhibition prior to any agreement with Nigerian officials. Only protests from the original excavator, Thurstan Shaw, led to contact with the Nigerian authorities and an accord to return the pot to Nigeria (if not to its proper resting place in Ibadan). Protest during the exhibition led to an agreement to add an anti-looting component to the exhibition (supplied by R.J. McIntosh and arranged by myself). Although myself and colleagues visited the exhibition several times during its later run, no one ever saw this installation of panels in place. Today, these panels may be seen at the *Mission Culturelle de Djenné* to which they were donated by the Royal Academy. The Royal Academy continues to claim that they were, indeed, exhibited in London (R. J. McIntosh pers. comm.).

Public awareness measures have included both films and museum exhibitions for display both within Africa and in Europe. Van Beek's *The African King* (1990) is perhaps the best known of these efforts showing the shameless behaviour of members of the antiquities industry and the damage their activities cause (McIntosh 1996). Less well-known is another Dutch effort by Van der Waals, screened principally in Mali, showing the data which can be gleaned from the controlled, scientific excavation of Malian tells or Togué. When this documentary first showed in Mali, I invited the hotel's own *antiquaire* into the lobby to watch. The next day the antiquities disappeared from his stand, although I have no idea how long they stayed away(!). Finally there is the *Vallées du Niger* exhibition, which more than any other comparable exhibition tried to make the case against looting and for cultural heritage management. This well-known event, made its way throughout Europe and West Africa, accompanied by a substantial catalogue and a smaller souvenir booklet with several powerful anti-looting vignettes (Devisse *et al.* 1993). However, despite its best intentions, it has been implicated in provoking increased looting at the Bura mortuary sites of Niger, due to the publicity the exhibition gave them ('Les Cavaliers du Niger' by R-P. Paringaux and E. De Roux; *Le Monde* 30 July, 1997). This has remained a thorny problem -- how to present Africa's past to the public, without inciting collectors into a feeding frenzy.

Finally, there is the issue of supporting legislation to ban the import or sale of looted African antiquities in foreign countries. The uneven implementation of UNESCO 1972 and UNIDROIT 1993 has meant little if any Western success against the antiquities trade. There have, however, been a few local successes. After lobbying by the local and foreign archaeologists of Mali and Malian officials, a US Customs ban on the importation of looted antiquities and ethnographic objects from the Niger River Valley and Bandiagara escarpment regions of Mali was implemented in September 1993 (Karoupas 1995). The ultimate effectiveness of this ban remains unclear, and some have questioned the will or ability of US Customs officials to effectively implement this ban (Shapiro 1995). Indeed, I question whether import bans -- reliant entirely on random searches -- will ever have more than a propaganda value. It would be far more interesting to make illegal the <u>sale</u> of looted African antiquities.

In the end, we cannot relax our efforts. Whether one agrees with them or not, look at the success animal rights protestors have had in keeping furs out of fashion. Let us hope our persistent interventions will keep Jenné terracottas off of private pedestals.

CONCLUSIONS

It is evident that the role of Africanist archaeologists has changed appreciably since the more 'research for its own sake' years of the 70s and 80s. This has been the result of pressure applied by both by the tragedy of large-scale looting, and a genuine desire on the part of most professionals to make their work meaningful to a broader community. To this end it is important that Western archaeologists eschew the 'short-termism' of brief research projects focused on bringing kudos to the scholar in the form of quick publications, choosing instead long-term commitments to countries and regions -- their people, their scholars and their heritage.

References

Bedaux, R. and M. Rowlands (2001). 'The Future of Mali's Past' *Antiquity* 75: 872-6.

Bedaux, R., K. MacDonald, A. Person, J. Polet, K. Sanogo, A. Schmidet, and S. Sidibé (2001). 'The Dia Archaeological Project: rescuing cultural heritage in the Inland Niger Delta (Mali)' *Antiquity* 75: 837-48.

Chippendale, C. (1991). 'Editorial' *Antiquity* 65: 823-30.

Dembélé, M. and J. Van der Waals (1991). 'Looting the Antiquities of Mali' *Antiquity* 65: 904-5.

Devisse, J., J. Polet and S. Sidibé (1993). *Vallées du Niger (souvenir booklet)*. Paris: SEPIA.

Healey, P. (1984). 'Archaeology Abroad: Ethical Considerations of Fieldwork in Foreign Countries'. In *Ethics and Values in Archaeology* (Green, E. ed.), New York: Free Press, pp. 123-32.

Inskeep, R. (1992). 'Making an honest man out of Oxford: Good news for Mali' *Antiquity* 66: 114.

Karoupas, M. (1995). 'US Efforts to Protect Cultural Property: implementation of the 1970 UNESCO Convention' *African Arts* 28/4: 32-41.

Kiethega, J. (1995). 'Regional Museums on Archaeological Sites'. In *Museums and the Community on West Africa*

(Ardouin, C. and E. Arinze eds.), Washington (DC): Smithsonian, pp. 50-9.

MacDonald, K. (1997). 'Korounkorokalé revisited: the *Pays Mande* and the west African microlithic technocomplex' *African Archaeological Review* 14: 161-200.

MacDonald, K., T. Togola, R. MacDonald and C. Capezza (1994). 'International news: Douentza, Mali' *Past: The Newsletter of the Prehistoric Society* 17: 12-14.

McIntosh, R. (1991). 'Resolved: to act for Africa's historical and cultural patrimony' *African Arts* 24/1: 18-22.

McIntosh, R. (1996). 'Just say shame: excising the rot of cultural genocide'. In *Plundering Africa's Past* (Schmidt, P. and R. McIntosh eds.), London: James Currey, pp. 45–62.

McIntosh, R., T. Togola and S. McIntosh (1995). 'The Good Collector and the Premise of Mutual Respect among Nations' *African Arts* 28/4: 60-9.

Shapiro, D. (1995). 'The Ban on Malian Antiquities: a matter of law' *African Arts* 24/1: 42-51.

Shaw, T. and MacDonald, K. (1995). 'Out of Africa and out of context' *Antiquity* 69: 1036-9.

7. MANAGING ON SCARCE RESOURCES: THE PAST RECORD, PRESENT SITUATION AND FUTURE PROSPECTS OF ARCHAEOLOGICAL RESOURCE MANAGEMENT IN LESOTHO

Peter MITCHELL

INTRODUCTION

Preserving and protecting archaeological resources is never easy, particularly given the financial stringency and infrastructural underdevelopment that prevail across so much of Africa. However, in few countries, perhaps, is this problem more acute than in Lesotho (fig. 7.1). Thirty-five years after independence Lesotho still lacks a functioning national museum and employs only one professionally trained archaeologist; most of the finds and archives relating to such fieldwork as has taken place is housed abroad. Though fewer than twenty sites have been excavated, spread across an area of 30,000 km^2, field surveys have identified many hundred more (table 7.1); some estimates place the number of rock art sites alone at in excess of 4000, the vast majority of them unrecorded (Smits 1991). This paper has several aims. Following a brief review of past research, it assesses the poorly developed state of Lesotho's archaeological infrastructure, identifies the main threats to the country's archaeological resources and considers some of the challenges posed by increasingly large-scale development projects. Finally, it sets out suggestions for actions that could (and should) be initiated to improve the management of Lesotho's archaeological heritage.

RESEARCH HISTORY

Lesotho's archaeology is almost entirely that of Bushman hunter-gatherers and their ancestors, the last of whom lost their independence, their livelihood and, in many cases, their lives as recently as the late nineteenth century (Vinnicombe 1976). Iron Age farming settlement within Lesotho's present boundaries began only in the seventeenth century and has scarcely been explored archaeologically, though much work has been undertaken on related sites in South Africa (e.g. Maggs 1976). Dreyer's (1996) excavations at Thaba Bosiu National Monument, capital of Lesotho's first king, Moshoeshoe I, are the sole example of professional Iron Age archaeological research within Lesotho. After an extended period of amateur activity concentrating on reporting stone artefact scatters and Bushman rock paintings and ethnohistory, systematic archaeological work began in the late 1960s (Mitchell 1992). Between then and now four major foci of activity can be identified, along with several smaller projects and others sponsored by UNESCO and the Lesotho Highlands Development Authority, both of which I discuss separately below. These major foci are:

1 - Rock art recording. Two projects stand out, though others, some conducted on shoestring budgets such as the recent work of Aitken *et al.* (2000) in the Lesobeng Valley, could also be cited. In the late 1960s Patricia Vinnicombe (1976) traced paintings in several areas of eastern Lesotho as part of a larger project extending into the KwaZulu-Natal Drakensberg; a separate survey was conducted in the lower Senqunyane Valley (Bousman 1988). This work was instrumental in reorienting southern African rock art research toward the ethnographically informed understanding that prevails today. On an even larger scale the ARAL (Analysis of the Rock Art of Lesotho) Project of Lukas Smits, formerly of the National University of Lesotho comprehensively recorded almost 700 sites between 1979 and 1986. With support from the Netherlands Foundation for the Advancement of Tropical Research, the Dutch Ministry of Development Co-operation and the Leverhulme Trust, the result was the creation of a massive archive of over 50,000 colour transparencies accompanied by detailed sketches (Smits 1973, 1983, 1992). Unfortunately, relatively little of this material has yet been published and only copies of the records for those sites along the Southern Perimeter Road and in Sehlabathebe National Park are held in Lesotho (Ambrose 2000).

2 - Eastern Lesotho. Vinnicombe's recording of rock sites formed part of the first large-scale, professional archaeological project to be undertaken in Lesotho and was conducted in collaboration with Pat Carter (1978), who pioneered investigations of the 'dirt' archaeology of Lesotho's Highlands. Through field survey and excavation at key sites (four in Lesotho and two in KwaZulu-Natal) he was able to construct base-line cultural-stratigraphic and palaeoenvironmental sequences for human settlement of the whole region during the late Quaternary (Carter 1976, 1978; Carter and Vogel 1974; Vogel 1983). Two of these sites, Sehonghong and Melikane, along with Pitsaneng, 1 km upstream from Sehonghong, contain paintings interpreted by a nineteenth century Bushman informant at a time when rock art itself was still being produced (Orpen 1874), information that was crucial to the development of a

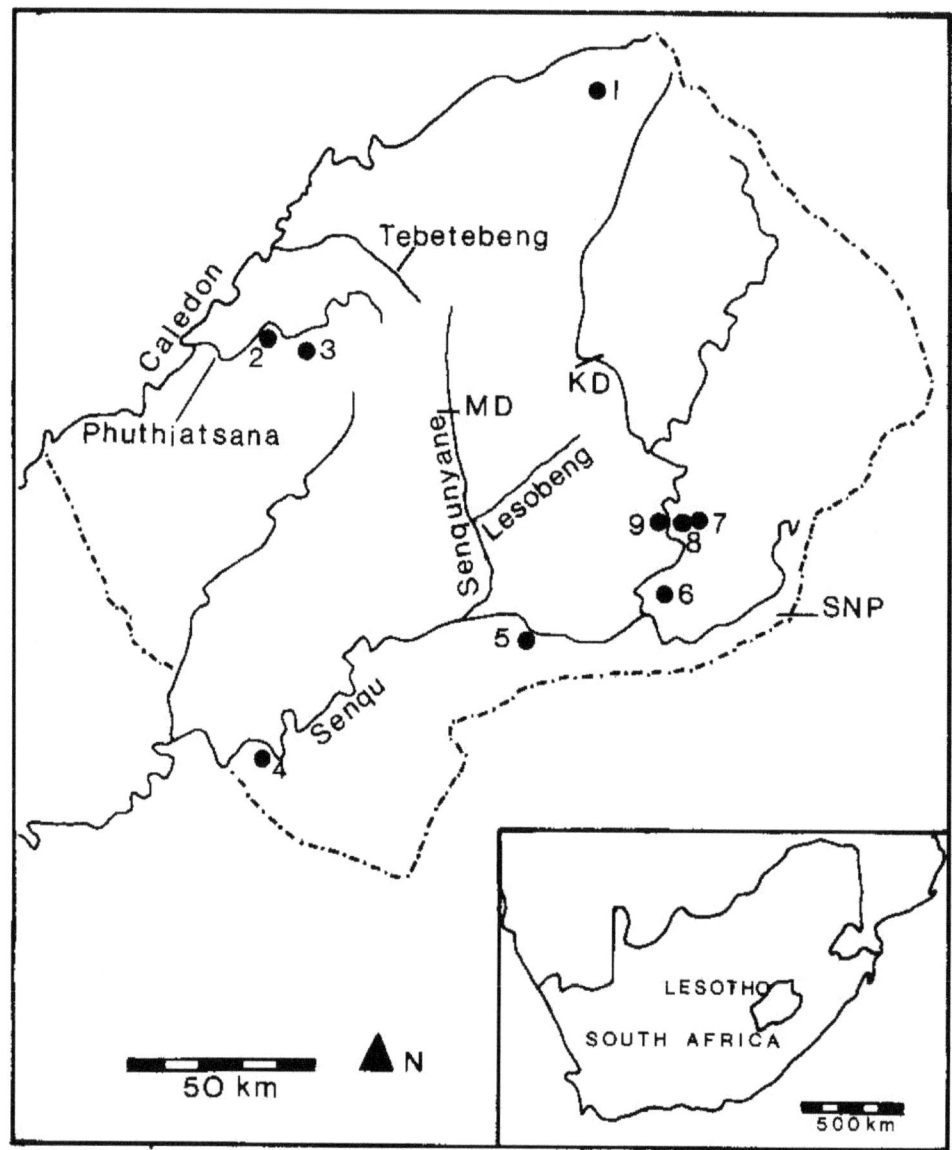

Fig. 7.1. Lesotho showing key sites and locations mentioned in the text. KD Katse Dam (Phase IA of LHWP); MD Mohale Dam (Phase IB of LHWP); SNP Sehlabethebe National Park. Archaeological sites: 1 Liphofung; 2 Thaba Bosiu; 3 Ha Baroana; 4 Masitise; 5 Bolahla; 6 Melikane; 7 Pitsaneng; 8 Sehonghong; 9 Likoaeeng

shamanistic understanding of Bushman rock art (Lewis-Williams 1981) and continues to provoke debate as this paradigm is reassessed (e.g. Jolly 1995; Solomon 1997). On a sub-continental scale, both Sehonghong and Melikane are also important for the completeness of their cultural-stratigraphic sequences: the former is one of literally a handful of sites with good faunal preservation occupied before at and after the Last Glacial Maximum (Deacon 1990), the latter one of very few to preserve Howieson's Poort assemblages within a longer Middle Stone Age sequence, again with well preserved faunal material (Carter 1978).

The Sehonghong area has also been the focus of more recent research. Sehonghong itself was re-excavated in 1992, producing a set of observations that provide a more highly resolved understanding of technological, subsistence and ecological change in the Lesotho Highlands over the past 25,000 years (Mitchell 1996a). This was accompanied by detailed survey of the surrounding area (Mitchell 1996b), in the course of which an important late Holocene open-air hunter-gatherer site was located at Likoaeeng. Two seasons of excavation have followed here (Mitchell and Charles 1996; 1998; 2000) and other sites have been test-excavated, while J. Hobart has excavated recently at Pitsaneng (J. Hobart, pers. comm.). Analysis of finds from all these sites is ongoing.

3. Southern Perimeter Road. Between the two episodes of fieldwork in the Highlands that I have just discussed, the 1980s saw important archaeological research in other parts of Lesotho. In the early part of the decade comprehensive impact assessment surveys were carried out ahead of construction of the Southern Perimeter Road (Parkington *et al.* 1987; Smits 1992) and two sites, Bolahla and Masitise, were excavated (Mitchell *et al.* 1994).

Table 7.1. Approximate numbers of archaeological sites recorded by major fieldwork projects in Lesotho

Project/director	Date	Painted sites	Other sites	References
P. Carter and P. Vinnicombe Eastern Lesotho	1969-74	177	56	Carter (1978); Vinnicombe (1976)
P. Vinnicombe Senqunyane Valley	1975	30	20	Bousman (1988)
L. Smits ARAL (several areas)	1979-86	668	-	Smits (1973; 1983, 1991; 1992)
J. Parkington et al. Southern Perimeter Road	1982-83	-	62	Parkington et al. (1997) Mitchell et al. 1994)
P. Mitchell Phuthiatsana Basin and adjacent areas	1988-90	76^1	46	Mitchell (1994)
LHDA Phase IA	1988-97	19	5	Lewis-Williams (1989); Loubser and Thorp (1993)
P. Mitchell Sehonghong area of the Senqu Valley	1992-98	8^2	65	Mitchell (1996b; unpublished fieldnotes)
LHDA Phase IB	1993-95	3	9	Parkington and Mitchell (1993); Kaplan (1995b)
British Schools Exploring Society Western bank of the Senqu Valley, Sehonghong to Lebakeng	1998	26	-	Ambrose (2000)
S. Aitken et al. Lesobeng Valley	2000	10	-	Aitken et al. (2000)
Approximate total		**1017**	**263**	

Notes
1 - Since some of the painted sites recorded in these areas are also included in the ARAL Project total sites recorded in the Phuthiatsana Basin and adjacent areas in 1988-90 and 1995 have been excluded from the total of painted sites at the bottom of the table.
2 - Many more rock art sites in this area were recorded previously by Carter (1978) and Vinnicombe (1976) and/or by ARAL. They are included in the totals given for these projects.

4. Phuthiatsana Basin. Subsequently, the period 1988-90 saw the first systematic investigation of the archaeology of Lesotho's lowlands. Mitchell (1994) carried out field surveys and excavated at four Later Stone Age sites in the Phuthiatsana Basin, as well as briefly surveying part of the Tebetebeng Valley to its north. Results complement those from more extensive work on the South African side of the Caledon River (Wadley 1995), allowing them to be placed within a broader regional context (Mitchell 2000).

THE PAST RECORD

Following on from a Proclamation (No. 40 of 1938) made during the colonial period for the preservation of historical monuments, rock paintings and other antiquities (Ambrose et al. 2000:105), provision was made even before Lesotho's independence for the establishment of a national museum (Khitsiane 1991). A 1967 Act of Parliament (Act No. 41) set up a Museum Board to develop such an institution, along with a Commission (commonly known as the Protection and Preservation Commission, or PPC) charged with protecting and preserving Lesotho's natural and cultural heritage (Ambrose 1983). This was further defined by Proclamation 36 of 1969 to include all rock engravings and paintings and all archaeological deposits in the country (Ambrose et al. 2000:107). Historically severely underfunded and under-resourced, the PPC has been able to do little to protect or preserve any of these, except for brief spells when it has benefited from external funding. An attempt to develop the well-known rock art site at Ha Baroana near Maseru failed, for example, for want of financial support. Short-lived improved tourist access to the site in the 1970s and 1980s actually accelerated damage to paintings as water was poured onto them in an attempt to improve their photogenic qualities, while the associated handicrafts operation collapsed, protective fencing was stolen and attendants left unpaid (Ambrose 1983).

Instead, the major contribution made by the PPC during its first 15 years or so was to lobby for the incorporation of an archaeological impact assessment in advance of the construction of a new road through the south of the country in the early 1980s (Ambrose 1983). The first such assessment conducted in Lesotho, this was undertaken by Lukas Smits' ARAL Project in relation to rock art and by the University of Cape Town, led by John Parkington, in relation to 'dirt archaeology'; well over 100 sites were recorded (Parkington *et al.* 1987; Smits 1992). Emboldened by this success, the PPC sponsored excavation of a rock-shelter demolished during construction of the Roma-Ramabanta road and was able to preserve some of the paintings from the site (Connally 1981; Ambrose 1983). Since the early 1980s, however, its capacity to function effectively has continued to be constrained by its minimal level of financial support. Lacking any inspectorate arm, the PPC's ability to license and monitor scientific research in Lesotho is limited. Several foreign-based researchers have simply ignored it (N. Khitsiane, pers. comm.), including more than one South African archaeologist.

The history of the National Museum is even more depressing. When finally constructed, it was pulled down in 1980 before it could open in order to make way for government offices (Khitsiane 1991). Another site was subsequently identified and architects have again recently been approached, but Lesotho remains one of the few countries without a national museum. As a result, there is nowhere to house or display excavated archaeological materials, nothing to act as a centre for archaeological research and no national focus for displaying Lesotho's heritage to tourists or, more importantly, its own citizens, especially schoolchildren. There has never been an archaeological presence at the National University of Lesotho and, while the Museum and Archives of the Lesotho Evangelical Church at Morija provide a partial substitute by way of research and education, this is a wholly private institution and again lacks a trained archaeological presence (Gill 1995). Indeed, with the exception of Taole Tesele, who is employed by the Lesotho Highlands Development Authority (of which more in a moment), no Mosotho has any professional archaeological training, or is in a position to undertake archaeological research. One further consequence is that all the fieldwork carried out in Lesotho thus far has been undertaken by expatriate researchers or by individuals based in Britain or South Africa. Furthermore, virtually all finds from that fieldwork, including the rock art archives built up by Patricia Vinnicombe and Lukas Smits, reside outside the country, either in South Africa, the United Kingdom or the Netherlands (table 7.2).

Table 7.2. Current location of major collections and archives from archaeological fieldwork in Lesotho

P. Vinnicombe   1967-76
Rock art tracings and notes, Senqu, Senqunyane and Tsoelike Valleys and other areas of the Eastern Highlands.
Rock Art Research Institute, University of the Witwatersrand, Johannesburg, South Africa.

P. Carter   1969-75
Excavated finds from Ha Soloja, Melikane, Moshebi's Shelter, Sehonghong and associated surface finds.
University Museum of Archaeology and Anthropology, Cambridge, United Kingdom.

L. Smits   1979-86
ARAL Project archive Ellecom, Netherlands.

J. Parkington   1982-83
Excavated finds from Bolahla and Masitise.
Department of Archaeology, University of Cape Town, South Africa.

P. Mitchell   1988-90
Excavated finds from Ha Makotoko, Mokhokhong, Ntloana Tsoana and Tloutle and associated surface finds from the Phuthiatsana Basin. Pitt Rivers Museum, University of Oxford, United Kingdom.

P. Mitchell   1992
Excavated finds from Sehonghong.
Department of Archaeology, University of Cape Town, South Africa/Pitt Rivers Museum, University of Oxford, United Kingdom.[1]

P. Mitchell   1995/98
Excavated finds from Likoaeeng and associated sites in the Senqu Valley. Pitt Rivers Museum, University of Oxford, United Kingdom.[1]

J. Hobart   2000
Excavated finds from Pitsaneng.
Pitt Rivers Museum, University of Oxford, United Kingdom.[1]

S. Aitken *et al.*   2000
Rock art photographs and notes, Lesobeng Valley.
Rock Art Research Institute, University of the Witwatersrand, Johannesburg, South Africa.

Note
1 - Still under study

The reasons for this state of affairs are not hard to find. Totally surrounded by South Africa, Lesotho has no significant natural resources, other than water and the labour of its people and continues to depend heavily for its economic well-being upon foreign aid and the remittances sent home by migrant workers (Gay et al. 1995). Beyond this, its political history since independence has included four coups, sporadic guerrilla activity, military and economic attacks by the former South African *apartheid* regime and a more recent (1998) South African-led military intervention. Taken together, this has not proven a favourable set of circumstances for spending significant sums on heritage protection at the expense of other sectors of government expenditure.

THE PRESENT SITUATION

The situation I have described has begun to alter over the past 12 years, partly as a result of the establishment of the Lesotho Highlands Water Project and partly because of a separate UNESCO-launched initiative focused around Thaba Bosiu. While contributing to an overall improvement in archaeological resource management, both developments also reveal important difficulties of approach that remain to be resolved. Indeed, they and other initiatives, such as the proposed Maloti-Drakensberg Transfrontier Conservation Area, also carry the risk of exacerbating the existing threats posed to the survival of Lesotho's archaeological resources.

Thaba Bosiu National Monument

Encouraged by the German Embassy and the United Nations Development Programme, UNESCO brought together a series of individuals and organisations at a conference in Maseru in 1991 to consider the future management of Lesotho's cultural heritage (Slotta and Skalli 1991). From an Africanist perspective, the choice of a British academic specialising in Roman archaeology, German scholars with experience of aerial photography in the Middle East and a French architect as the best informed individuals to take a leading rôle in these deliberations was puzzling, to say the least. Nevertheless, something positive was achieved in that a small site museum was developed at the base of Thaba Bosiu. This helps introduce the site to tourists, regulates access to it and preserves a number of historically significant items, including some associated with King Moshoeshoe I. As part of the same UNESCO project, excavations were undertaken on the top of Thaba Bosiu in 1995 by Kobus Dreyer, at that time an archaeologist of the National Museum, Bloemfontein, South Africa. Intriguingly, his work suggests that Thaba Bosiu was occupied even before Moshoeshoe I's arrival there in 1824 (Dreyer 1996). Further investigations were, however, curtailed because of sensitivities relating to the presence on the mountain's summit of the graves of Lesotho's royal family. They have not been resumed.

The Lesotho Highlands Water Project

The Lesotho Highlands Water Project, one of the largest development projects currently underway in Africa, seeks to impound water along several of Lesotho's rivers for transfer to the rapidly growing and industrialising greater Johannesburg area of South Africa. As well as developing its infrastructure, Lesotho gains financially from selling water to South Africa and economically from generating electricity for its own consumption, thereby reducing its dependence on its larger neighbour (Mitchell in press). Designed in several phases, with each phase adding to the transfer capacity of earlier ones, the ultimate transfer of $70m^3$ of water per second will only be achieved on the project's completion. This will require construction of at least four, possibly as many as six, dams linked by tunnels that ultimately feed into South Africa's Vaal River system. If completed in its entirety, the outcome will be the transformation of the landscape of the Lesotho Highlands, though not without attendant economic, social and ecological costs (Gay et al. 1995; International Rivers Network 2000; 2001).

On a positive note, the Lesotho Highlands Development Authority (LHDA), the para-statal body responsible for implementing the scheme within Lesotho, has, after a shaky start, acted to ensure that the claims of archaeology are considered. In the Phase IA area, which includes the Katse Dam (finished in 1998) and the Muela hydroelectric station with its attendant reservoir, this has involved extensive field survey, detailed recording of threatened rock art sites, the removal for safekeeping of paintings of exceptional scientific value and excavations at two rock-shelters (Lewis-Williams and Thorp 1989; Mitchell and Parkington 1990; Loubser 1993; Kaplan 1995a). A third rock-shelter was also partially excavated, and had its paintings recorded in detail, as part of a programme to develop it as a local museum (Kaplan 1992). Historically associated with Moshoeshoe I (Arbousset 1991), Liphofung has now become a flagship project for LHDA's heritage management activities (Ambrose et al. 2000). The second stage of the Highlands Water Project, Phase IB, involves construction of the Mohale Dam on the uppermost reaches of the Senqunyane River, the anticipated completion date for which is 2003. Here LHDA has sponsored further archaeological survey and excavation in the areas to be flooded (Kaplan 1995b, 1996), as well as initiating surveys along possible new road alignments (Parkington and Mitchell 1993).

There is, however, a downside to all of this. To begin with, almost all of the archaeological work undertaken at LHDA's behest remains unpublished; details of only one excavation (Mitchell et al. 1994) and two rock art sites (Lewis-Williams and Dowson 1990; Loubser and Brink 1992), all in the Hololo Valley, have yet appeared in print. The remainder of the archaeology of Phases IA and IB continues to languish in the almost wholly inaccessible 'grey literature' to which so much contract archaeology seems condemned, effectively inaccessible to other archaeologists. A second concern is that almost all the fieldwork undertaken since 1990 has been carried out by a small, private contract archaeology operation, inevitably lacking the resources of a major museum or university department. It is also unclear how much, if any, of this work has been carried out with the permission of, or in liaison with, the PPC, the relevant statutory body for licensing and monitoring scientific research in Lesotho.

A third difficulty with LHDA's plans for managing the impact of its activities on Lesotho's archaeological heritage relates to the development of an appropriate archaeological infrastructure. To be sure, this is by no means a problem or responsibility unique to LHDA. Nevertheless, despite the successive recommendations of the Project's original Feasibility Study (Lehmeyer Macdonald and Olivier Shand 1986), its first two archaeological consultants (Lewis-Williams and Thorp 1989) and its own Draft Environmental Action Plan (LHDA 1989), remarkably little has been done. Technical assistants remain unrecruited, storage and laboratory space for the analysis and curation of finds insufficient. The one positive development, the professional training (to B.A. (Hons) level) of LHDA's archaeologist, Mr T. Tesele, owed much another source, the generous funding by the Wenner Gren Foundation of a scholarship at the University of Cape Town. Though widely acknowledged as an excellent field archaeologist and rock art recorder (his previous experience lay with the ARAL Project), he has, regrettably from an archaeological standpoint, subsequently spent a considerable amount of time on wholly non-archaeological matters.

Happily, none of these difficulties has mattered too much thus far, and the overall level of archaeological work undertaken by LHDA has been broadly commensurate with its impact on archaeological sites. Should, however, Phase III (let alone Phases IV and V) of the Project ever be built the situation will be completely different. All three of these dams will flood extensive areas of sandstone along the main Senqu Valley, areas known to be rich in archaeological sites, with many more not yet identified, and almost all uninvestigated. To give some idea of the scale of the problem, flooding of an 8.5 km stretch of the Senqu River near Sehonghong will drown at least 40 sites (Mitchell 1996b and unpublished fieldnotes). Sixteen are open-air Middle and/or Later Stone Age artefact scatters, seventeen have rock paintings (six with associated artefact scatters) and six are unpainted rock-shelters with artefact scatters. Several of these shelters contain archaeological deposits, while the remaining site, Likoaeeng, is a buried rock-shelter turned open-air campsite. The quality of its faunal preservation, which includes evidence of a massive investment in fishing, combined with its highly resolved multi-component stratigraphic sequence, makes this site alone significant on a sub-continental scale (Mitchell and Charles 2000). Scaling these figures up for the entire Phase III area suggests that hundreds of archaeological sites will be lost forever should dam construction take place. In addition, many others will be at massively increased risk of vandalism. These include not only the three Orpen-recorded rock art sites of Sehonghong, Pitsaneng and Melikane, but also a rare example of a multi-component Middle Stone Age rock-shelter in the Likonong Valley with ten superimposed occupation levels and good faunal preservation (Mitchell unpublished fieldnotes).

The tragedy of LHDA's archaeology programme is that this is completely foreseeable: the PPC's report to Government for 1982 when the Project was first under consideration, the 1986 Feasibility Study (Lehmeyer Macdonald and Olivier Shand 1986), the initial impact assessment by David Lewis-Williams and Carolyn Thorp (1989), and LHDA's (1989) own Draft Environmental Action Plan all demanded comprehensive reconnaissance and survey work in the Phase III area *at least* ten years before construction begins. Nothing has been done to set this in motion, despite the fact that construction of the Phase III Dam on the Tsoelike River was initially intended to commence in 2013! Furthermore, instead of adopting the advice of the original Feasibility Study to set up an independent Lesotho Heritage and Scientific Research Organisation (Lehmeyer Macdonald and Olivier Shand 1986: C-3: 7.3; C-5: 13), LHDA has handled archaeology through its Environmental Division, the principal responsibilities of which lie in rural development, compensation, resettlement and public health.

These shortcomings are not so surprising, given that the entire Lesotho Highlands Water Project was initiated without a comprehensive environmental impact assessment being undertaken. Only *after* work had begun did South Africa and Lesotho agree in 1990 to produce an Environmental Action Plan, leading to a full environmental impact assessment being carried out for Phase IB and the establishment by the World Bank, one of the Project's major donors, of a panel of experts to assess implementation of agreed action plans (Ledger 1996). Continuing intergovernmental discussions and a lack of long-term commitment from international donors may cast doubt over the future of the Lesotho Highlands Water Project, but, whatever the impact of water conservation measures within South Africa, it is difficult to see how else the greater Johannesburg area can secure access to sufficient water for its future needs. The problem that this poses for Lesotho's archaeology is that it seems more than likely that only when a firm decision is taken to proceed with further phases of the Project will thought be given to initiating additional archaeological fieldwork. Inevitably, this will be too late for such fieldwork to be undertaken on the scale required.

OTHER THREATS AND POSSIBILITIES

These remarks only reinforce the threat hanging over Lesotho's archaeology from other sources. On the one hand there is the ongoing problem posed by a variety of destructive processes. These are most in evidence with rock art: paintings may be damaged by or for tourists when water or other liquids are thrown over them to enhance (temporarily!) their colours; by local people, particularly children, writing or drawing over paintings in charcoal; by removal of ochre for use in traditional medicines; and by animals rubbing against painted surfaces or stirring up dust. Beyond all of these, the rock faces on which the paintings exist are themselves friable and subject to exfoliation (Loubser 1991; Meiklejohn 1994). There are no definitive estimates of the rate at which rock art is disappearing in Lesotho because of these processes, but anecdotal evidence and comparative data from KwaZulu-Natal (Ward 1997) demonstrate that this is a serious problem that demands action if the majority of the surviving paintings are not lost without record. Rock art is almost certainly the component of Lesotho's archaeological heritage most susceptible to loss. In the absence of a ready market for LSA pottery or for stone tools, other archaeological resources are far less endangered. Since very few rock-shelters are inhabited today and kraal construction within them rarely, if ever, impacts sub-surface deposits, the major ongoing threat is that posed by building works and normal agricultural activity, especially ploughing, to the integrity of open-air artefact scatters.

This is not to suggest that other dangers do not exist. Indeed, the other side of this equation is constituted by the challenges and, to be fair, the opportunities posed by major development projects. Across Lesotho these include the upgrading of existing road networks, for which archaeological impact assessments are frequently conspicuous by their absence. Take, for example, the recent (1999) construction of a new road across the Sehonghong Valley as part of the link between the two regional centres of Thaba Tseka and Qacha's Nek. Though this goes within metres of Sehonghong Shelter itself (J. Hobart, pers. comm.), no consideration appears to have been given to its possible impact on open-air sites in the immediate locality, still less to the protection of Sehonghong's paintings from increased visitor access. A longer-term challenge comes from the suggestion that much of the Phuthiatsana Valley be drowned in order to create a reservoir capable of supplying Maseru, Lesotho's capital. Not only is this area scenically very beautiful, it includes important areas of arable land and a wealth of archaeological sites (Smits 1983; Mitchell 1994). For none of these have rock paintings been adequately traced, while excavations are limited to a total of 11 m^2 in two of the largest shelters, which include deposits dating to the Pleistocene/Holocene transition that are of more than just local significance (Mitchell 1993a; Mitchell and Steinberg 1992); the rest of the Valley's archaeology is unknown.

Currently, much attention is being given to another development initiative which, at least in principle, should be more beneficial to archaeology. This concerns the development, over five years and at an estimated cost in excess of US$ 15,000,000, of a joint Lesotho-South Africa Trans-Frontier Conservation Area (TFCA) in the Maloti Mountains and along the Drakensberg Escarpment. As one of several Peace Parks now being developed in southern Africa, the Lesotho component of it stands to profit from both international funding and co-operation with South African researchers, but negotiations for its implementation are still continuing between one important donor, the World Bank, and South Africa (Maloti-Drakensberg Trans-frontier Conservation Area 2000). Provided that the TFCA is developed with the informed participation and consent of local communities (*pace* the initial phase of the Basotho Pony Project; Ferguson 1990), it may offer an important means by which they can obtain tangible benefits from the region's rich archaeological heritage. But for this to be possible, community involvement in supervising visitor access and providing tourists with appropriate information and guidance will be essential. This points up the importance of developing the future management of Lesotho's archaeological heritage in a sustainable way.

FUTURE PROSPECTS

Where might Lesotho go from here? Firstly, international donors, and in the case of the Highlands Water Project this definitely includes the South African government, need to take archaeology seriously, fund survey and excavation appropriately, ensure that they are done competently, and provide opportunities for training Basotho as archaeologists. The World Bank, which has helped fund both the Lesotho Highlands Water Project and intends to fund the TFCA initiative, is increasingly emphasising such a position as it re-evaluates its responsibilities as a development donor. But external funding sources, however, important, cannot be a long-term substitute for locally generated revenue. As Mabulla (1996) advises for Tanzania, this must come from a variety of sources, including tourism receipts that are ploughed back into heritage management, greater direct government provision and developer funding. For the latter to be effective, Lesotho needs to follow the example of other southern African countries, such as Botswana (Phaladi 1998), and require environmental impact assessments in advance of all major developments, even where these are not funded or demanded by international donors. And for this to work, the PPC, in turn, must have an effective, adequately funded inspectorate, while developers, architects, engineers and government officials need to be made aware of their legal responsibilities to Lesotho's archaeological heritage (Mabulla 1996; Phaladi 1998).

Secondly, a national archaeological database needs to be constructed and maintained (for example, by the PPC) to provide a baseline for heritage management (Slotta and Skalli 1991: 76; Mitchell 1993b). Though copies of some field survey archives are housed with the PPC (e.g. for Mitchell's work in the Phuthiatsana Basin and the Sehonghong area of the Senqu Valley), this is not invariably the case. Duplication of the ARAL Project's archives, in particular, is a pressing need, but will require substantial funds to be raised. Only when such a national database of archaeological sites has been created, with appropriately trained and equipped staff to maintain it, can Lesotho develop a coherent strategy for the protection and preservation of its archaeological heritage. Sufficient goodwill and sense of responsibility exists on the part of those who have conducted fieldwork there to ensure that their records form part of this database, and all future field projects should be required to do the same.

Thirdly, archaeology and other components of Lesotho's heritage need to be involved in both public education and tourism initiatives. That the Government is now moving once more in the direction of constructing a National Museum is extremely welcome, and it is to be hoped that it will provide an opportunity for displaying at least some of the finds from the past thirty-five years of archaeological fieldwork. Equally, greater efforts need to be made to present the results of such fieldwork to local communities.

The enthusiasm shown by local schools, for example, when visiting recent excavations at Likoaeeng, Pitsaneng and Sehonghong indicates the interest that there is among the population at large. Two ways of taking this further would be for archaeologists to provide Sesotho language booklets to schools and local communities reporting on the results of their work and, following in the wake of South Africa's recent education reforms (Esterhuysen 2000), for archaeology to be introduced into primary and secondary school curricula. Botswana's travelling museum, which attempts to visit all schools every few years and introduce pupils to archaeological finds and methodologies, offers another means of attaining the same goal (Pule 1998).

A fourth suggestion goes to the heart of much of what I have discussed since it combines issues of heritage management, revenue generation and community participation. Worldwide, culturally and ecologically sensitive tourism is undergoing an explosive period of growth. Though it cannot boast the early hominid sites and major game reserves of a South Africa or a Tanzania (Mabulla 2000), Lesotho nevertheless combines spectacular scenery, an outstandingly rich rock art heritage, a population well disposed to foreign visitors and a varied bird and plant life, along with excellent opportunities for fishing, hiking and pony-trekking. The Sehonghong/Melikane stretch of the Senqu Valley alone could easily attract several hundred, or even thousand, tourists a year who would, by local standards, pay well for the privilege of visiting it. Much more could be done to market these attractions within southern Africa. Much more could also be done further afield, though since few overseas visitors come specifically to Lesotho, this might be best undertaken in conjunction with South Africa. The Maloti-Drakensberg Transfrontier Conservation Area could be important here (cf. Wahl *et al.* 1998), but such initiatives also require more 'joined-up government' on the part of the Lesotho authorities to ensure that cultural heritage management, wildlife conservation and tourism are organically linked. The time should be long past when, for example, a National Park can be proclaimed, but left outside the remit of the National Parks Act to be managed by too small a staff located on the opposite side of the country (Ambrose *et al.* 2000: 79; 110).

From both archaeological and community development standpoints it is essential that tourism be built as much from the bottom up as from the top down. The Basotho Pony Project based at Molimo-Nthuse has had real success in generating income for local communities from the supply of guides, accommodation, food and fuel, and might provide a model for similar ventures that could incorporate an archaeological dimension. Community-based initiatives in other parts of Africa may also offer valuable guidance (Holt-Biddle 1994; Pwiti and Mvenge 1996; Pwiti 1997; Pule 1998; Mabulla 2000). Critically important elements include the involvement of local people in project management and the upgrading or construction of local facilities (e.g. roads, site museums), as well as the provision of clear economic benefits through employment as guides and interpreters or the sale of handicrafts (baskets, hats, or even store-bought blankets). Above all, money generated from tourism *must* be ploughed back into heritage management and into local communities. Only in this way will it be possible to ensure that local people take charge of and see value in Lesotho's archaeological heritage, particularly rock art, its most threatened component. Only in this way will it be possible to ensure that paintings are protected from further damage and that the impact of growing numbers of visitors is regulated and managed for the benefit of archaeology and local people alike. Only if such programmes, and the other suggestions made above, can be developed in a low cost, and ultimately locally sustainable, form will they have any real prospect of improving on the past situation that I have described.

Acknowledgements

I am grateful to the Protection and Preservation Commission of the Kingdom of Lesotho for having given me permission to conduct my own fieldwork in Lesotho and to all those Basotho who have helped make that fieldwork such a worthwhile and enjoyable experience. I hope that the suggestions made in this paper can be realised to their benefit. Thanks too to all those colleagues and students who have worked with me in successive seasons and to Gloria Ruggieri for having improved this paper by reading through it before its submission.

References

Aitken, S., Q. Lake, N. Mills, and M. Moshoeshoe (2000). *Lesotho Rock Art Survey 2000*. Report submitted to the Protection and Preservation Commission of the Kingdom of Lesotho.

Ambrose, D. (1983). *Lesotho's Heritage in Jeopardy*. Maseru: Protection and Preservation Commission of the Kingdom of Lesotho.

Ambrose, D. (2000). *Lesotho Annotated Bibliography: Section 132 Rock Paintings*. Roma: National University of Lesotho Institute of Education.

Ambrose, D., E. Motebang Pamela, and S. Talukdar (eds.) (2000). *Biological Diversity in Lesotho*. Maseru: National Environment Secretariat of Lesotho.

Arbousset, T. (1991). *Missionary Excursion into the Blue Mountains* (ed. Ambrose, D. and A. Brutsch). Morija: Morija Museum and Archives.

Bousman, C. (1988). 'Prehistoric settlement in the Senqunyane Valley, Lesotho' *South African Archaeological Bulletin* 43: 33-37.

Carter, P. (1976). 'The effects of climatic change on settlement in eastern Lesotho during the Middle and Later Stone Age' *World Archaeology* 8: 197-206.

Carter, P. (1978). *The Prehistory of Eastern Lesotho*. Unpublished Ph.D. thesis, University of Cambridge.

Carter, P. and J. Vogel (1974). 'The dating of industrial assemblages from stratified sites in eastern Lesotho' *Man* 9: 557-570.

Connally, M. (1981). *The Excavation of the Roma Rock Art Site (ARAL A11)*. Report submitted to the Protection and Preservation Commission of the Kingdom of Lesotho.

Deacon, J. (1990). 'Changes in the archaeological record in South Africa at 18 000 BP'. In *The World at 18 000 BP. Volume*

Two: Low Latitudes (Gamble, C. and O. Soffer eds.), London: Unwin Hyman, pp. 170-188.

Dreyer, J. (1996). 'Thaba Bosiu: mountain fortress of Lesotho'. In *Guide to Archaeological Sites in the Free State and Lesotho* (Brink, J., J. Dreyer, Z. Henderson and S. Ouzman eds.), Bloemfontein: Southern African Association of Archaeologists, pp. 37-46.

Esterhuysen, A. (2000). 'The birth of educational archaeology in South Africa' *Antiquity* 74: 159-165.

Ferguson, J. (1990). *The Anti-Politics Machine: 'Development', Depoliticization and Bureaucratic State Power in Lesotho*. Cambridge: Cambridge University Press.

Gay, J., D. Gill and D. Hall (eds.) (1995). *Lesotho's Long Journey: Hard Choices at the Crossroads*. Maseru: Sechaba Consultants.

Gill, S. (1995). *A Guide to Morija*. Morija: Morija Museum and Archives.

Holt-Biddle, D. (1994). 'Campfire: an African solution to an African problem' *Africa: Environment and Wildlife* 2/1: 33-3.

International Rivers Network (2000). http://www.irn.org/programs/lesotho. Accessed 8th June 2001.

International Rivers Network (2001). http://www.irn.org/wcd/lhwp.shtml Accessed 8th June 2001.

Jolly, P. (1995). 'Melikane and upper Mangolong revisited: the possible effects on San art of symbiotic contact between south-eastern San and southern Sotho and Nguni communities' *South African Archaeological Bulletin* 50: 68-80.

Kaplan, J. (1992). *Archaeological Excavations at Liphofung Cave*. Report submitted to the Lesotho Highlands Development Authority.

Kaplan, J. (1995a). *The Archaeology of the Muela Rock-Shelter*. Report submitted to the Lesotho Highlands Development Authority.

Kaplan, J. (1995b). *Archaeological Reconnaissance of Mohale and Matsoku*. Report submitted to the Lesotho Highlands Development Authority.

Kaplan, J. (1996). *Archaeological Excavations at Lithakong Shelter (SQY 8)*. Report submitted to the Lesotho Highlands Development Authority.

Khitsiane, N. (1991). Efforts in the preservation of cultural heritage in Lesotho. In *International Symposium on Preservation and Presentation of the Cultural Heritage of Lesotho* (Slotta, R. and M. Skalli eds.), Bochum: German Mining Museum, pp. 36-8.

Ledger, J. (1996). The Lesotho Highlands Water Project and the Environment. In *Vision of Wildlife, Ecotourism and the Environment in Southern Africa* (Ledger, J. ed.), Johannesburg: Endangered Wildlife Trust, pp. 94-99.

Lehmeyer Macdonald Consortium and Olivier Shand Consortium (1986). *Lesotho Highlands Water Project Feasibility Study. Supporting Report C: Environmental and Social Impact in Lesotho*. Maseru: Government of Lesotho.

LHDA (Lesotho Highlands Development Authority) (1989). *Lesotho Highlands Water Project - Phase IA: Draft Environmental Action Plan*. Maseru: Lesotho Highlands Development Authority Environment Division.

Lewis-Williams, J. (1981). *Believing and Seeing: Symbolic Meanings in Southern San Rock Paintings*. Cambridge: Cambridge University Press.

Lewis-Williams, J. and T. Dowson (1990). 'Through the veil: San rock paintings and the rock face' *South African Archaeological Bulletin* 45: 5-16.

Lewis-Williams, J. and C. Thorp (1989). *Archaeology: Lesotho Highlands Water Project Environmental Study*. Report by Environmental Resources Ltd, London, submitted to the Lesotho Highlands Development Authority.

Loubser, J. (1991). 'The conservation of rock paintings in Australia and its applicability to South Africa' *Navorsinge van die Nasionale Museum, Bloemfontein* 7: 113-143.

Loubser, J. (1993). *Provisional Report on the Conservation of Fourteen Painted Rock Shelters Affected by Phase IA of the Lesotho Highlands Water Project*. Report submitted to the Lesotho Highlands Development Authority.

Loubser, J. and J. Brink (1992). 'Unusual paintings of wildebeest and zebra-like animals from north-western Lesotho' *Southern African Field Archaeology* 1: 103-107.

Mabulla, A. (1996). 'Tanzania's endangered heritage: a call for a protection program' *African Archaeological Review* 13: 197-214.

Mabulla, A. (2000). 'Strategy for cultural heritage management (CHM) in Africa: a case study' *African Archaeological Review* 17: 211-234.

Maggs, T. (1976). *Iron Age Communities of the Southern Highveld*. Pietermaritzburg: Natal Museum.

Maloti-Drakensberg Transfrontier Conservation Area (2000). http://www.maloti.org.za. Accessed 8th June 2001.

Meiklejohn, K. (1994). *Aspects of the Weathering of the Clarens Formation in the KwaZulu-Natal Drakensberg: Implications for the Preservation of Indigenous Rock Art*. Unpublished Ph.D. thesis, University of Natal, Pietermaritzburg.

Mitchell, P. (1992). 'Archaeological research in Lesotho: a review of 120 years' *African Archaeological Review* 10: 3-34.

Mitchell, P. (1993a). 'Archaeological investigations at two Lesotho rock-shelters: the terminal Pleistocene/early Holocene assemblages from Ha Makotoko and Ntloana Tsoana' *Proceedings of the Prehistoric Society* 59: 39-60.

Mitchell, P. (1993b). 'A national archaeological database for Lesotho' *National University of Lesotho Journal of Research* 3: 67-83.

Mitchell, P. (1994). 'The archaeology of the Phuthiatsana-ea-Thaba Bosiu Basin, Lesotho, southern Africa: changes in Later Stone Age regional demography' *Antiquity* 68: 83-96.

Mitchell, P. (1996a). 'The late Quaternary of the Lesotho Highlands, southern Africa: preliminary results and future potential of ongoing research at Sehonghong Shelter' *Quaternary International* 33: 35-44.

Mitchell, P. (1996b). 'The late Quaternary landscape at Sehonghong in the Lesotho Highlands, southern Africa' *Antiquity* 70: 623-38.

Mitchell, P. (2000). 'The organization of Later Stone Age lithic technology in the Caledon Valley, southern Africa' *African Archaeological Review* 17: 141-176.

Mitchell, P. (in press). 'Archaeology and the Lesotho Highlands Water Project'. In *Damming the Past*, (Brandt, S. and F. Hassan eds.), Lexington: Lexington Books.

Mitchell, P. and R. Charles (1996). 'Archaeological investigation of an open air hunter-gatherer site in the Lesotho Highlands: preliminary report on the 1995 season at Likoaieng' *Nyame Akuma* 45: 40-49.

Mitchell, P. and R. Charles (1998). 'Archaeological fieldwork in the Lesotho Highlands, July and August 1998: the second season of excavation at the Likoaeng open-air site' *Nyame Akuma* 50: 13-21.

Mitchell, P. and R. Charles (2000). 'Later Stone Age hunter-gatherer adaptations in the Lesotho Highlands, southern Africa'. In *Human Ecodynamics: Proceedings of the Conference of the Association of Environmental Archaeology*

(Bailey, G., R. Charles and N. Winder eds.), Oxford: Oxbow Press, pp. 90-99.

Mitchell, P. and J. Parkington (1990). *The Archaeology of the Hololo Crossing Rock-Shelter*. Report submitted to the Lesotho Highlands Development Authority.

Mitchell, P., J. Parkington and R. Yates (1994). 'Recent Holocene archaeology in western and southern Lesotho' *South African Archaeological Bulletin* 49: 27-56.

Mitchell, P. and J. Steinberg, (1992). 'Ntloana Tsoana: a Middle Stone Age sequence from western Lesotho' *South African Archaeological Bulletin* 47: 26-33.

Orpen, J. (1874). 'A glimpse into the mythology of the Maluti Bushmen' *Cape Monthly Magazine* 9: 1-13.

Parkington, J. and P. Mitchell (1993). *Archaeological Impact of Road Construction in the Phase IB Area of the Lesotho Highlands Water Project*. Report submitted to the Lesotho Highlands Development Authority.

Parkington, J., R. Yates and C. Poggenpoel (1987). *Lesotho Rescue Archaeology 1982/83*. Cape Town: University of Cape Town.

Phaladi, S. (1998). 'The organisation of archaeology'. In *Ditswa Mmung: The Archaeology of Botswana* (Lane, P., A. Reid and A. Segobye eds.), Gaborone: The Botswana Society, pp. 233-239.

Pule, T. (1998). 'Archaeology and museums'. In *Ditswa Mmung: The Archaeology of Botswana* (Lane, P., A. Reid and A. Segobye eds.), Gaborone: The Botswana Society, pp. 240-248.

Pwiti, G. (1997). 'Taking African cultural heritage management into the twenty-first century: Zimbabwe's masterplan for cultural heritage management' *African Archaeological Review* 14: 81-84.

Pwiti, G. and G. Mvenge (1996). 'Archaeologists, tourists and rainmakers: Problems in the management of rock art sites in Zimbabwe'. In *Aspects of African Archaeology* (Pwiti, G. and R Soper eds.), Harare: University of Zimbabwe Publications, pp. 817-24.

Slotta, R. and M. Skalli (eds.) (1991). *International Symposium on Preservation and Presentation of the Cultural Heritage of Lesotho*. Bochum: German Mining Museum.

Smits, L. (1973). 'Rock paintings in the upper Senqu Valley, Lesotho' *South African Archaeological Bulletin* 28: 32-38.

Smits, L. (1983). 'Rock paintings in Lesotho: site characteristics' *South African Archaeological Bulletin* 38: 62-76.

Smits, L. (1991). 'Rock paintings in Lesotho'. In *Lesotho, Kingdom in the Sky* (Giesen, J. ed.), Berg en Dal: Afrika Museum, pp. 199-206.

Smits, L. (1992). 'Rock painting sites near the Southern Perimeter Road in southeastern Lesotho'. In *Rock Art in the Old World* (Lorblanchet, M. ed.), New Delhi: Indira Gandhi National Centre for the Arts, pp. 61-95.

Solomon, A. (1997). 'The myth of ritual origins ? Ethnography, mythology and interpretation of San rock art' *South African Archaeological Bulletin* 52: 3-13.

Vinnicombe, P. (1976). *People of the Eland*. Pietermaritzburg: University of Natal Press.

Vogel, J. (1983). 'Isotopic evidence for past climates and vegetation of South Africa' *Bothalia* 14: 391-394.

Wadley, L. (1995). 'Review of dated Stone Age sites recently excavated in the eastern Free State, South Africa' *South African Journal of Science* 91: 574-579.

Wahl, E., A. Mazel and S. Roberts (1998). 'Participation and education: developing a cultural resource management plan for the Natal Drakensberg Park, KwaZulu-Natal, South Africa' *Natal Museum Journal of Humanities* 10: 151-170.

Ward, V. (1997). 'A century of change: rock art deterioration in the Natal Drakensberg, South Africa' *Natal Museum Journal of Humanities* 9: 75-97.

8. EGYPTIAN CULTURAL HERITAGE MANAGEMENT: LET'S WORK TOGETHER

Geoffrey TASSIE

"The strength of Egypt is in its fathomless heart. He who appeals to the heart of Egypt, gives it back its soul"
(Fekri A. Hassan 1998: 206, citing Al-Hakim from *'Awdat Al-Rouh*).

INTRODUCTION

Egypt's cultural heritage (which may be defined in broad terms as being: elements of past material culture, music, dance or oral tradition that may have meanings and values placed upon them by present populations) is one of the richest, most varied and ancient in the world, encompassing the whole story of the human achievement. Palaeolithic cultures, state formation, the growth of the Persian, Greek, Roman and Arab empires are all represented within Egypt's borders, along with Egypt's Pharaonic past. Today, such archaeological sites and monuments all over Egypt are threatened by a number of factors: urban sprawl, infrastructure development projects, agricultural expansion, pollution and looting. The large number of sites and monuments, as well as the countless artefacts in museums and storerooms, all requiring constant monitoring, protection and maintenance, are more than Egypt's financial capabilities can bear (Hassan 1997: 90).

However, although Egypt is rich in cultural heritage *sensu lato*, it is too idealistic to suggest that the entire materiality of the past be preserved (Skeates 2000: 17). Therefore, a selective policy must be undertaken as to which elements are to be preserved (Ucko 1992). In the past, this policy – especially at the international scale -- has generally focused on preserving the stone-built monumental buildings of the Pharaonic and Graeco-Roman eras (UNESCO World Heritage Sites; see Hassan 1997: 88; Skeates 2000: 11-16). Clearer policies for the selection of a representative sample of material from all periods must be formulated, so that it may be recorded, preserved and protected, based on the nature and extent of the total archaeological database (Skeates 2000: 17-18). To select a sample of the cultural heritage of Egypt (and therefore effectively protect it) it is important to know the extent, whereabouts and amount of archaeological sites in Egypt. However at present there is no National Register or central Sites and Monuments Record (SMRs) for Egyptian cultural heritage, and the databases that do exist are unconnected islands of information lacking any central organisation.

The area of ownership of Egypt's cultural heritage is generally considered as a two-way relationship, for as Vittorini Veronese, a former Director-General of UNESCO stated when raising funds for the Nubian Rescue Campaign in the 1960s, these "wonderful structures, ranking among the most magnificent of earth" do not belong solely to the countries which hold them in trust. The whole world has a right to see them endure. They are part of a common heritage "entitled to universal protection" (cited by Chamberlain 1979: 178). However, it has fallen to Egypt's governmental organisation, the Supreme Council of Antiquities (SCA) to take the major responsibility to care for the vast quantity of cultural heritage within Egypt's boarders (Hassan 1997: 90). The SCA has a long and varied history, with its roots in Egypt's colonial past, a past that did little to prepare the present organisation for the colossal task that it now faces, especially in regards to training schemes for professional Egyptian field archaeologists (Reid 1984). Egyptology is primarily a 'western' discipline, fostered principally by the French and British, with the Germans and Italians joining in during the mid-nineteenth century, and by 1900 Russia and the USA had also commenced Egyptological exploration. However this 'Western' Egyptology, the traditional discipline as originally conceived in the light of epigraphic and historical rather than archaeological study, sought to either commandeer Egypt's heritage as part of a European historical narrative or construct an exotic, oriental, 'other', fostering schizophrenic and opposing cultural identities.

THREATS TO EGYPT'S HERITAGE AND CONFLICTING INTERESTS

The following non-exhaustive list details some of the prime threats to Egypt's cultural heritage (after Skeates 2000: 39):

1) Acid rain and normal weathering processes
2) Pollution
3) Modern agricultural practices and land reclamation
4) Looting
5) Demolition, building and development projects
6) Urban encroachment as a result of overpopulation.
7) Earthquakes, floods and other natural disasters
8) Tourism
9) Deterioration caused by a change of environment owing to archaeological excavation
10) Salinization
11) Rise in water table levels
12) Lack of money and resources
13) *Sebakhin* (fertiliser extraction)
14) Raw material extraction

15) Military training areas
16) Construction of dams
17) Seismic movement

Many of these factors are exacerbated by a lack of central investment. Let us now assess, in more detail, the nature and potential impact of these threats.

Although sites and monuments all over Egypt are at risk, the Nile Delta is the region that is most acutely threatened by many of the factors outlined above, as highlighted by many of the SCA's officers and other scholars at a session in the *Eighth International Congress of Egyptologists* (see Tassie, Rowland and de Trafford 2000). Destructive forces at work on the heritage of the Delta include mainly: salinization, mechanical farming techniques and agricultural intensification, land reclamation (involving flooding of large tracts of land), pollution, rising water tables, *Sebakhin* (other threats, as outlined above are also present in varying degrees). The Delta region is therefore widely recognised as being an exceptionally at-risk archaeological environment (e.g. Spencer and Spencer 2000; Theroux 1997; el-Wakil 1988). The increasing need by farmers for more arable land is pressing the archaeological sites ever more; Brink (1986: 7-8) expanded on some of these threats to the archaeological sites of the Delta:

1. The main rural building material is mud-brick; and *kom* (tell) soil is frequently used for manufacturing these mud-bricks. In several cases, Brink noticed that brick factories comprising of up to 10 kilns were located on a *kom*. With the rapid increase of the rural population, and the villages themselves rapidly expanding, more mud-bricks are required. In May 1985, a law came into action to prevent this, only granting licenses to brick making factories that acquire their material by dredging the canals. However, this law is proving hard to enforce.

2. Owing to the shift from basin irrigation to perennial irrigation and the consequential intensification of land-use, as well as land reclamation, there has been a rise in the impoverishment of the soil. The *kom* soil with its high fertiliser content is being taken to feed the crops in the fields.

3. Many of the geziras (island settlements rising above the flat flood plain) have been used as sand quarries, therefore destroying possible settlement remains.

4. A law which forbids houses to be built on agricultural land has meant that the Egyptian Ministry of Agriculture is urging the SCA to investigate areas that are under its protection as quickly as possible, so that they can be turned over for land reclamation. The assessment of these sites is made by way of soundings, although only the topmost (and therefore most recent strata) are investigated in this manner.

Within the Delta sites where there were once great mounds (*koms*), there are now only fields or only half a mound, many having been ploughed away. "Some of the *tells*, particularly the small ones or those near modern towns and cities, have been levelled for agricultural purposes or swallowed up by urban development" (Spencer and Spencer 2000: 26). Another major problem is the lack of trained personnel and resources to help stem the problem; as Rabie el-Kasim points out the excavations at Silvago are hampered by the lack of a site photographer and conservator, and although there is no mention of the lack of a physical anthropologist, it seems one was absent from the excavation of this cemetery site (el-Kasim 1988: 279-80). El-Kasim (1988: 280) goes on to point out that in the area of Marsa Matrouh, research would be greatly helped by the use of a *Land Rover*, fuel, water tanks and access to a good compass; all are sadly lacking. Mohammed Bakr (1982: 154) of the University of Zagazig, noted the following situation at the ancient city of Bubastis (modern Tell Basta) also known as the mound of cats:

"the urban expansion of Zagazig has resulted in the loss of some parts of the archaeological site which now lies under modern buildings. In the race with the modern development of the town, the Zagazig University has formulated a project for the safeguard of the ancient site which is the witness of many events leaving their mark on its earth over the long history of Ancient Egypt".

This problem is common to many sites in the Delta. Even at sites that are nominally protected, vandalism and looting still occurs. On a recent visit to the ancient city of Tanis, the effects of *Sebakhin* could clearly been seen on the great mud-brick walls of the city, much of which still lies beneath large unexcavated mounds (Tassie *pers. obs.*). This is not an isolated instance, and it occurs all over Egypt owing to pressure for more arable land. Other instruments of danger to sites are caused, not by direct action, but indirect action, such as the irrigation of fields in areas adjacent to archaeological sites; this usually has the effect of making the mean water table level rise and also allows chemical fertilisers to leech into the 'protected' archaeological standing remains.

Keeping areas out of cultivation indefinitely is neither practical nor desirable; the Delta -- and Egypt as a whole -- cannot be kept as a permanent open-museum, and neither should it be. However, if a site has been fully excavated and published and is not going to be exhibited and if the land is required by local farmers, should it stay out of cultivation indefinitely? This question is too large to be answered here, but the issue must be raised and a committee of world experts should debate this question as part of a larger Delta project. Can we afford to 'write-off' heritage in this way? It is the wish of the Egyptian Ministry of Agriculture that these 'non-productive' areas of land be turned over to the farmers as quickly as possible, and therefore a complete and comprehensive survey of the Delta is of the utmost importance, not only for the archaeological information that can be gained, but so that the modern burgeoning Delta population can produce the food and other materials it so desperately needs.

These conflicts of interest, between farmers, developers, industrialists, hoteliers, governmental bodies and archaeologists and conservators, are sadly commonplace.

The current population of Egypt is rising by a about one million people every year; a middle ground must be sought to protect, conserve and record the archaeological resources, whilst not impeding the growth potential of modern Egypt.

Archaeologists should be aware of local environmental issues and pressures, and try to cooperate with the farmers in land and water management, as well as disseminating their results to the local population. There needs to be a building of trust between the archaeologists and the public; many local farmers in Egypt are often too fearful to report any archaeological finds on their land although they are compelled to do so by Law 117. As Ede (1995: 213) notes: "It is reported that if a farmer hands in a find, his land is likely to be removed from cultivation until full excavation has been carried out (a lengthy process which he obviously cannot afford). If he sells it, and is caught, he faces a long period in jail. As a result, we have heard that many pieces are simply being thrown in the Nile". This is a real no-win situation all round.

Archaeologists themselves are also directly responsible for damaging the very monuments they seek to study (see also Larocca this volume); John and Elizabeth Romer have blamed uncaring Egyptologists for much of the recent damage done to the tombs in the Theban Hills, especially those in the Kings' Valley (1993). The Romers (1993: 39-72) cite many examples of damage done to tombs, particularly that of Seti I (recently conserved by the American Research Center in Egypt; see Jones 2000: 93-4), however, the major problem is that many of the Egyptologists working in these tombs, conducting epigraphic work and 'tomb clearance', have limited archaeological, conservation and cultural heritage management knowledge or skills and this is entirely a result of 'traditional' Egyptology training. As el-Wakil (1988: 265) notes, the lack of detailed published reports from previous excavations, can also seriously hamper present and future archaeological research (also see Fagan 1996a).

The threats of water level rise to Egypt's heritage is considerable, and it takes a number of forms. Although the building of the Aswan High Dam and creation of Lake Nasser provided many benefits to the Egyptian population, its building constituted a major threat to Nubian cultural heritage, and many side-effects of its construction still threaten Egypt's cultural heritage. The creation of Lake Nasser, which is over 300 miles long, resulted in many Nubians being displaced and the majority of archaeological sites in the region being flooded (Romer and Romer 1993: 116-8), yet more far reaching is the problem that the change in the water regime has meant resultant change to irrigation patterns, and a rise in the water-table has led to the permanent soaking and weakening of the foundations of many ancient monuments forcing corrosive salts through their walls (Romer and Romer 1993: 118). In the Delta the building of the Aswan High Dam, and the consequent prevention of the yearly inundation which deposited its silt and washed the salt from the soil (and allied to the fact that the west Delta is sinking at 3 mm per year) has resulted in a general rise in the groundwater and salination levels (Theroux 1997: 8-9). However, at the *Eighth International Congress of Egyptologists*, Gamal El-Bouhy proposed the use of a computerised system in order to record the movement of water and fix its level to that below the archaeological buildings, until more permanent means of protection can be secured (El-Bouhy 2000: 38). At least we are beginning, in some small way, to address the problem.

Tourists, or rather irresponsible tourism, are another threat to Egypt's cultural heritage, inadvertently bringing with them erosion, pollution, noise and demands for amenities, such as rest houses, toilets, transport, entertainment, souvenir shops and accommodation (Skeates 2000: 61). The tourist industry in Egypt brings in $4.3 billion per year, one of the biggest earners of foreign revenue for the Egyptian Government (ISDC 2001; Skeates 2000: 61). However, within some government and religious circles, antiquities are viewed as nothing more than just this, a source of tourist dollars offering a threat to traditional Islamic values from rampant Western consumerism (Reid 1984: 246; Saadawi 1997: 161). The mass tourist industry is causing great damage to many of the monuments, and various examples of this can be seen in the Kings' Valley. Not only do backpacks inadvertently rub against the painted walls of tombs as tourists squeeze by one another, some tourists often bribe the guards to take flash photography of the ancient and fragile wall paintings, and it often happens that they will even pick up potsherds, or other archaeological material for souvenirs. The moist breath of the tourists allied to the vibration and diesel exhaust fumes from tourist buses entering the Valley have accelerated the damage to many of the tombs, and even sewage water leaking from an old septic tank in the old rest house found its way into tomb KV 5, causing extensive and very preventable damage (Romer and Romer 1993: 59-64). Although changes have recently been made, such as stopping tour buses from going right into the Kings Valley, the repair of the sewage tank and limiting the number of tourists that can see each tomb, it is clear that education of the tourists is still needed in the quest to prevent further damage to these beautiful, unique tombs.

One means of mitigating mass tourism at sites such as Giza and Luxor is for tour operators to offer tours to the less well-known sites. Recently there has been a rise in cultural and eco-tourism by smaller tour operators. However, the increase in tourism -- especially to sites that in the past have rarely been visited -- means that the local communities need to be taught how best to deal with this increase, and how they might fiscally benefit from tourism. Therefore a programme of public archaeology and site management must be implemented by the SCA and should be components in the plans of every expedition working in Egypt.

PROTECTING EGYPT'S CULTURAL HERITAGE: LEGISLATION AND COLLABORATION

The Egyptian law governing archaeology and the antiquities trade is Law no. 215 (31st October 1951) on the *Protection of Antiquities*, revised by laws no. 529 of 1953, no. 24 of 1965 and no. 117 of 1983. The Egyptian Government is preparing new legislative measures to compliment the already existing legislation. These measures will be supported by the following measures: adjustment of fees from tourists visiting the monuments to provide money for additional conservation, along with additional central funding from the Egyptian government; collaboration with international bodies in major conservation projects; adoption of environmental conservation to replace restorative conservation; multi-disciplinary cooperation; upgrading conservation research facilities; and an initiation of a programme to increase public awareness of Egypt's cultural heritage (Hassan 1997: 90). This is part of a larger plan initiated by His Excellency Farouk Hosny, Minister of Culture, who in 1993 formulated the following measures to assist in the protection of Egypt's cultural heritage:

1) Inventory and determination of the condition of archaeological remains to include test excavation and surveying.
2) Documentation of monuments and archaeological sites.
3) Determination of the environment of sites and monuments to minimise or prevent natural and human-induced threats and hazards.
4) Restoration and preservation of monuments.
5) Establishing a database of the condition and history of conservation of monuments.
6) Dissemination of archaeological knowledge to enhance public awareness and to involve the public in conservation efforts.

(Translated from Arabic by Hassan 1997: 91).

The training of personnel capable of carrying out these measures was high on his list of priorities. Field schools therefore need to be established immediately throughout Egypt to train Egyptian personnel in the fundamentals of modern archaeological field methods and to set standards of documentation, cultural heritage management, conservation, and to encourage cooperation and dissemination of knowledge. A conference held in the North Sinai Research Centre, Qantara, organised by Peter Ucko (the *Egyptian Human Remains: Retrieval, Conservation and Analysis* Conference in April 2000) was one of the first steps toward the training of personnel in modern archaeological practice (Mower and Tassie 2000). It is hoped that a programme of training can now be established under the auspices of this centre. Another step was the holding of a UNESCO Training Programme at the East Delta site of Kafr Hassan Dawood, under the directorship of Fekri Hassan. This collaborative project trained many Egyptian and Western students in modern field methods and techniques (Hassan 2000). Training programmes are also run by the American Research Centre Egypt and the Italian Centre for Restoration and Archaeology. However, these efforts must be increased and expanded, couched within a larger scheme of international cooperation and perhaps a national school of archaeological evidence established for the training of personnel in CHM.

For cultural heritage management to be truly effective in Egypt, large-scale capacity building, in terms of both personnel and resources, needs to be undertaken. The first step in effective cultural heritage management is in establishing a well-equipped and trained antiquities service, with a smoothly running infrastructure. The SCA of Egypt has such a large infrastructure, but crucially the lack of funding and resources is sometimes critical, especially at the local inspectorate level (Reid 1984: 246). The teaching of proper archaeological methodology and implementation of minimum standards is even more acutely needed (Mower and Tassie 2000). There is a real lack of Egyptology books in Arabic (most are written in the one of the three traditional languages of Egyptology - English, French or German; Reid 1984: 235). Although many Egyptian Inspectors speak English fluently, technical books in Arabic are needed to explain many of the specific terms used in archaeology in their own language. Moreover, many of the books in foreign languages are just not available to the vast majority of Inspectors, unless they visit Chicago House at Luxor or approach institutions in Cairo. Training staff and producing Arabic books are two of the easiest and most cost-effective methods that can be implemented immediately.

The Egyptian Cultural Heritage Organisation (ECHO), a non profit, non-governmental organisation dedicated to assisting Egypt in preserving and managing its cultural heritage, is in the final stages of production of the *Field Handbook of Excavation Methodology and Recording Techniques: Standards and Conventions* (Tassie in prep.). This book although initially written in English will have an Arabic counterpart. Some of the more modest and simple actions that can be taken by the international institutions and missions working in Egypt are: disseminating their results of the research to the public and cultural heritage community, devoting time to educate the local inspectors about their archaeological project and the methods used, including young Egyptian archaeologists and scientists in their team, and fuller active collaboration with the SCA (Hassan 1997). Modern Egyptians, although custodians of this heritage, should therefore not be solely burdened with the task of maintaining it, and funding from international bodies needs to be secured. Only by working together toward a common goal can archaeology in Egypt truly move forward.

TOWARDS A CENTRAL SMR

One of the most efficient ways of meeting Farouk Hosny's priorities, is the establishment of a National Register or a central Sites and Monuments Records. The creation of a National Register (computerised relational database) will allow the protection of sites and monuments to be conducted more effectively because it will help define the amount of cultural properties in Egypt and make planning and development easier, as the information will be readily available to all interested parties (see also Finneran this volume). At present, the information is scattered in different databases or non-existent, and the central records that do exist are hand-written in a free-text format with an attached location map and photograph, but no serial number. A central archive with standardised recording or nomination forms must be created to hold all the archival information and original documentation created by surveys and excavations. This must be closely aligned with the development of a National Register, which lists all the cultural properties in Egypt.

The first step in creating a National Register is defining what constitutes a cultural property. Within Law 117, a cultural property is defined as any movable or immovable property that is a product of any of the past civilisations from prehistoric times to 100 years before the present (although there are special provisions for cultural properties of less than 100 years to be identified as an antiquity). The second stage in creating a National Register is knowing, the whereabouts, extent and state of preservation of these cultural properties. In the case of Egypt, a survey of the literature to date is an essential in creating a National Register, to assess the condition, environment and history of conservation of the sites and monuments already surveyed or excavated. To complement the survey of the documentary evidence a survey and assessment of the state of preservation of the Egypt's sites and monuments should be carried out in the field, monitoring closely the causes and threats of damage to cultural properties. To do this standardised recording forms need to be created, stating the information required in the National register. An archaeological survey of Egypt must be instigated, with endangered areas, such as the Delta, the Red Sea Coast, North Sinai, along the edge of the Nile Floodplain and reclamation areas in the oases, receiving highest priority (Hassan 1997: 91). There have already been many surveys done, such as the Theban Mapping Project, and those conducted in the Delta (Bietak 1975; Brewer *et al.* 1996; Brink 1988; Brink *et al.* 1986; Chlodnicki *et al.* 1998; Coulson 1988; Holladay 1982; Spencer and Spencer 2000; Wunderlich 1988), these must be collated and integrated into the central Survey of Egypt Project as the initial stage in creating a National Register. To this end, dissemination of archaeological and technical knowledge from around the world is essential, and working groups should be set up, as well as training centres, to help in this process. All the institutions involved in archaeological work in Egypt, especially those that have already completed or are engaged in survey work should be invited to a dedicated conference on CHM to agree a common methodological strategy. After the initial gathering of information on sites and monuments a 'sites and monuments at risk' project should be established to conduct fuller surveys and excavation of those sites deemed to be most at risk as well as to continuously monitor and actively preserve and protect Egypt's heritage, both legislatively and physically.

The surveying of Egypt and the creation of a National Register is a long term project, probably taking 20 years to complete the initial stages; it took 500 people in Poland 13 years to complete a survey of 65% of the total area and log the information into the Polish Archaeological Records (Jaskanis 1992). However, an innovative project directed by Fathi Saleh, and backed by UNESCO and the SCA, is the foundation of the Ministry of Communication and Information Technology, which has in collaboration with the SCA established the National Centre for Documentation of Cultural and Natural Heritage (CultNat). The creation of the 'Archaeological Map of Egypt' is a pilot scheme designed by the centre to produce a national archaeological map of Egypt, implementing GIS and database technology to record Egypt's cultural heritage. The purpose of the map is to create a sites and monuments' inventory and incorporates other archaeological and museum databases from around the world. So far, 300 sites have been included with bibliographic references for each site (Saleh and Grimal 2000:160). The map is also linked to the Egyptian Museum catalogue to show site relevant artefacts that are housed in the museum. This scheme is the first real attempt at a Sites and Monuments Records (SMRs) for Egypt and will hopefully be supported by the wider community of Egyptologists. CultNat is also documenting Egypt's natural heritage, musical heritage, folklore, photographic heritage and Cairo's architectural heritage in a computerised database (www.cultnat.org).

Developmental controls are part and parcel of the raison d'être of the SMR. One way to mitigate the effects of urban sprawl and large development projects is to introduce archaeological assessments and watching briefs (as happens in the UK), couched within new legislation that compels the developers to alert the SCA of their projects and provide funding for archaeological work (Skeates 2000: 74-6). However, this new legislation will be 'intimately linked to questions about the appropriate levels of and details of site recording programmes, environmental impact statements, and rescue excavations' (Ucko 1992). Measures taken could include local Inspectors making laptop assessments before conducting an on-the-ground survey to assess the amount and type of archaeology present, if any, before the commencement of any building programme. When foundations of a building are being dug, Inspectors could make a watching brief, and halt proceedings if any archaeological remains are found, in order that they may make a fuller assessment. Although archaeological assessment work is being carried out at present to a limited degree, the training of personnel able to conduct this type of work is essential along with legislation stating the required amount of test pits, standard of publication, etc.

Other ways of protecting Egypt's cultural heritage are by instigating a treasure act policy (see Skeates 2000: 42-3) and by formulating developmental plans for tourism that minimise the environmental and urban hazards and promote community involvement, including site management (Hassan 1998). Renfrew (2000 *passim*) proposes that the only long-term means of stopping looting is by changing public attitudes toward it by enhancing public concern and involvement and by the moral shaming of collectors and dealers in looted antiquities. The public must support a scheme that makes it no longer socially acceptable to collect or display looted antiquities (see also 1996b).

PRESENTING EGYPTIAN CULTURAL HERITAGE

Cultural heritage management, is still often seen as part of the archaeological process (Skeates 2000: 7-8). Archaeologists and museum curators must understand that they can no longer assume that Egypt's cultural heritage is their intellectual property, and that they are its sole guardians, and that they are the only ones who have the right to interpret this heritage (Skeates 2000: 36). The cultural and symbolic importance of the archaeological resource for nationalist narratives and tourists, among others, must also be taken into account (Hassan 1998: 201; Skeates 2000: 18). Western Egyptologists in particular must realise that they have to share Egypt's cultural heritage with Egyptian archaeologists, tourists and all the other interested parties, even if some of the interested parties give alternative or opposing interpretations of the material. Therefore, there must be more cultural sensitivity, consultation, mutuality, compromise and dissemination of knowledge, as this can only be beneficial for all the stakeholders (Skeates 2000: 37). An aware, responsible and engaged global archaeology should be a relevant, positive force, which recognises and celebrates difference, diversity and real multivocality.

For over two hundred years Egyptologists have not only been claiming the right to study and interpret Egypt's heritage on the public's behalf, but also to expect to be supported by them in doing so (Skeates 2000: 109). Archaeologists must bear in mind that, the preservation of the cultural heritage is not just for future generations of archaeologists to study and interpret but realise that there are many stakeholders in Egypt's cultural heritage. The present and future local and global public may wish learn from, enjoy and appreciate the ingenuity of past human achievements. This is best illustrated in the following quote: 'The problem confronting archaeology today is an acutely moral one. Access and presentation of the past in everyday life, not just in museums and at archaeological sites, is crucial in shaping our future' (Ucko 1990a). Although a lot of public and private money is granted to archaeologists to carry out their work (Schadla-Hall 1999), many archaeologists, both Egyptian and Western, are grossly underpaid for the amount of time and effort that they devote to the subject, many having to take additional jobs to supplement their meagre income from archaeology. Many good arguments have been put forward to support the position of archaeologists, (see Hassan 2001: 404-6; Skeates 2000: 109-10), but do they justify and guarantee the public's continued support, and what segments of society are being reached? Who is excluded?

The majority of people that visit heritage sites in Egypt are well-educated Western tourists, well-educated middle-class Egyptians or local school children (Hassan 1998). In some sections of the Egyptian community there is an indifference to Egypt's Pharaonic monuments, which is compounded by the fact that the Pharaonic past is often portrayed as being pagan, tyrannical and irrelevant to modern Islam (Hassan 1998; Saadawi 1997; Wood 1998). Interest in all Egypt's heritage can help galvanise the self-identity of the Egyptians whilst also helping to forge a new globalism. The management of Egypt's cultural heritage can help foster the role of objects in the cultural memory, show how the monuments have helped to forge a self-identity. The stable political future of Egypt depends upon an ability to integrate its pasts and reconcile its Pharaonic, Hellenistic, and Islamic heritage, and to place that varied heritage within the narrative of global civilization (Butler 1999: 53; Hassan 1998: 212). The contributions to humanity of Egypt's various pasts, including the Pharaonic past and Islamic past, must be presented to the Egyptian public and school children in a range of cultural and educational activities, within places of learning, museums, art galleries, works of literature, academic books, outreach projects and in architecture, it must be integrated into their everyday lives, showing Egypt's impact on globalism.

According to Hills (1993) it is mainly those already interested in the subject, whom are predominately well educated, middle-aged, middle-class people that watch documentaries and read the publications about ancient Egypt. This is the same group of people that predominately visit heritage sites and attend educational classes (Ucko 1990b). Many heritage sites in Egypt are not particularly visitor friendly, the sites of Tanis and Bubastis in the Delta do not have any information boards telling the tourist what they are looking at, neither do they have a guide book, this state of affairs can be found at many heritage sites throughout Egypt. Although the majority of tourists will have their own tour guides, visitors like to have a souvenir of the site and often like to read about what they are seeing during and after they have visited the site. Having adequate site management at the various archaeological sites throughout Egypt, even the less well-known sites, is one of the most effective methods of solving this problem.

As Ucko (1989) points out, archaeologists are still insufficiently attuned to their audiences cares and concerns. Archaeologists need to be aware of what the general public currently thinks about the profession and the past; they need to effectively communicate their findings to this large and predominately non-academic audience (Stone 1989). Archaeologists must engage in dialogue with the stakeholders, ask the individuals, groups and communities about what they want out of their heritage, how they would like it presented and preserved (Skeates 2000: 118). The popular must be embraced along with the academic, providing the public with much greater physical and mental access to the cultural heritage and archaeologists' work. Archaeologists need more input into popular television programmes on archaeology and to produce more popular books, with the aim of dispelling many of the myths and misconceptions that have sprung up about ancient Egypt. In learning about ancient Egypt, the public like to see golden treasure, a mummy or skeleton, scientific wizardry, but above all they like to know about what they did, how people lived, the clothes and hairstyles they wore, what they ate and made, especially the roles of woman and children, and how the past relates to and affects our lives in the present (Hills 1993; Skeates 2000: 121). Therefore, cultural heritage managers and museum curators must try and cater for the publics needs when putting on a museum display, by creating multimedia and interactive exhibits, allowing more access to their collections, creating travelling exhibitions to schools and libraries, taking the visitor on a process of self-discovery. Recently the Egyptian Museum in Cairo has put their collection on a database, which is accessible to the public. More on-site museums and visitor centres need to be created housing the artefacts that were excavated at that site, with relevant information for the public (see Finneran this volume). A Master Plan was created for the Giza plateau and its monuments (the Pyramids) in the early 1990s (see Mabbit 1992 and Evans and Fielding 2000), however, at present the plan is still someway from completion, and the visitors experience to the site will only really start to improve once the visitor flow is regulated more effectively and their knowledge of the site and pyramids in general is improved by the building of the three recommended visitor centres. This is surely a positive step in working together, on many levels, to promote Egypt's cultural heritage.

References

Bakr, M. (1982). 'New excavations of Zagazig University, Colloques internationaux du C.N.R.S. No. 595' *L' Egyptologie en 1979: Axes Prioritaties de Recherches* 1: 153-167.

Bietak, M. (1975). *Tell ed-Dab'a II.* Vienna: Verlag der Österreichischen Akademie der Wissenschaften.

El-Bouhy, G. (2000). 'Protective solutions to preserve antiquities from environmental factors.' In *Abstracts of Papers for the Eighth International Congress of Egyptologists* (Hawass, Z. and A. Jones eds.), Cairo: American University in Cairo Press, pp. 38.

Brewer, D., R. Wenke, J. Isaacson and D. Haag (1996). 'Mendes regional archaeological survey and remote sensing analysis' *Sahara* 8: 29-42.

Brink, E. (1988). 'The Amsterdam University Survey Expedition to the North-eastern Delta'. In *The Archaeology of the Nile Delta: Problems and Priorities* (Brink, E. ed.), Amsterdam: Netherlands Foundation for Archaeological Research in Egypt, pp. 65-114.

Brink, E., B. Wesemael and P. Dirksz (1986). 'A geo-archaeological survey of the North-Eastern Nile Delta, Egypt: the first two seasons, a preliminary report' *Mitteilungen des Deutsches Archäologisches Institut Kairo* 43: 7 -31.

Butler, B. (1999). 'Alexandria revived: new realizations of an ancient city' *Archaeology International* 2: 51-3.

Chamberlain, E. (1979). *Preserving the Past.* London: J. M. Dent.

Chlodnicki, M., R. Fattovich and S. Salvatori (1998). 'The Italian Archaeological Mission of the C.S.R.L. -Venice to the eastern Nile Delta: A preliminary report of the 1987 - 1988 field seasons'. In *Proceedings of the Seventh International Congress of Egyptologists, Cambridge 1995* (Eyre, J. ed.), Leuven: Peeters, pp. 45-62.

Coulson, W. (1988). 'The Naukratis Survey'. In *The Archaeology of the Nile Delta: Problems and Priorities* (Brink, E. ed.), Amsterdam: Netherlands Foundation for Archaeological Research in Egypt, pp. 259-263.

Ede, J. (1995). 'The antiquities trade: towards a more balanced view'. In *Antiquities Trade or Betrayed: Ethical and Conservation Issues* (Tubb, K. ed.), London: Archetype, pp. 211-14.

Evans, K. and L. Fielding (2000). 'Giza (Egypt): The use of GIS in managing a World Heritage Site'. In *Visitor Management: Case Studies from World Heritage Sites* (Shackley, M. ed.), Oxford: Butterworth-Heinemann, pp. 81-99.

Fagan, B. (1996a). 'Archaeology's dirty secret'. In *Archaeological Ethics* (Vitelli, K. ed.), London: Altamira, pp. 247-251.

Fagan, B. (1996b). 'The arrogant archaeologist'. In *Archaeological Ethics* (Vitelli, K. ed.), London: Altamira, pp. 238-243.

Hassan, F. (1997). 'The cultural heritage of Egypt: a world legacy'. In *African Cultural Heritage and the World Heritage Convention: Second Global Strategy Meeting,* Addis-Ababa: UNESCO, pp. 86-91.

Hassan, F. (1998). 'Memorabilia: archaeological materiality and national identity in Egypt'. In *Archaeology Under Fire, Politics and Heritage in the Eastern Mediterranean and Middle East* (Meskell, L. ed.), London: Routledge, pp. 200-16.

Hassan, F. (2000). 'Kafr Hassan Dawood' *Egyptian Archaeology* 16: 37-9.

Hassan, F. (2001). 'African archaeology: the call of the future' *African Affairs* 100 /398: 393-406.

Hills, C. (1993). 'The dissemination of information'. In *Archaeological Resource Management in the UK: An Introduction* (Hunter, J. and I. Ralston eds.), Stroud: Alan Sutton, pp. 215-24.

Holladay, J. (1982). *Cities of the Delta - Part 3: Tell el-Maskhuta. A Preliminary Report on the Wadi Tumilat Project 1978-79.* Published under the auspices of the American Research Center in Egypt.

IDSC (2001). *Egypt's Tourism Statistics.*
Online at http://www.idsc.gov.eg/tourism/min_sts.htm.

Jaskanis, D. (1992). 'Polish national record of archaeological sites - general outline'. In *Sites and Monuments: National Archaeological Records* (Larsen, C. ed.), Copenhagen: National Museum of Denmark, DKC, pp. 81-87.

Jones, M. (2000). 'The work of the American Research Center in Egypt in the Tomb of Seti I'. In *Late Abstracts of Papers for the Eighth International Congress of Egyptologists* (Hawass, Z. and A. Jones eds.), Cairo: American University in Cairo Press, pp. 93-4.

Mabbit, R. (1992) *The Masterplan for the Giza Plateau.* Paris: The Conservation Practice UNESCO.

Mower, J. and G. Tassie, G. (2000). 'Egyptian Human Remains: Retrieval, Conservation and Analysis: A Conference held at Qantara, Egypt, 25th-27th April 2000' *Papers from the Institute of Archaeology* 11: 116-124.

Reid, D. (1984). 'Indigenous Egyptology: the decolonization of a profession?' *Journal of the American Oriental Society* 105: 233-246.

Renfrew, C. (2000). *Loot, Legitimacy and Ownership.* London: Duckworth.

Rivers, J. (2000). 'Thebes (Luxor, Egypt): Traffic and visitor flow management in the West Bank Necropolis'. In *Visitor Management: Case Studies from World Heritage Sites* (Shackley, M. ed.), Oxford: Butterworth Heinemann, pp. 161-181.

Romer, J. and E. Romer (1993). *The Rape of Tutankhamun.* London: BCA.

Saadawi, N. (1997). *The Nawal el-Saadawi Reader.* London: Zed Books.

Saleh, F. and N. Grimal (2000). 'Carte archéologique de l'Egypte'. In *Late Abstracts of Papers for the Eighth International Congress of Egyptologists* (Hawass, Z. and A. Jones eds.), Cairo: American University in Cairo Press, p. 160.

Schadla-Hall, T. (1999). 'Editorial: public archaeology' *European Journal of Archaeology* 2/2: 147-58.

Skeates, R. (2000). *Debating the Archaeological Heritage.* London: Duckworth.

Spencer, J. and P. Spencer (2000). 'The Delta Survey' *Egyptian Archaeology* 16: 25-7.

Stone, P. (1989). 'Interpretations and uses of the past in modern Britain and Europe. Why are people interested in the past? Do experts know or care? A plea for further study'. In *Who Needs the Past? Indigenous Values and Archaeology* (Layton, R. ed.), London:Unwin Hyman, pp. 195-206.

Tassie, G. in Press. 'The Egyptian Cultural Heritage Organisation', *ECHO Newsletter* 1.

Tassie, G., J. Rowland and A. de Trafford (2000). 'The 8th International Congress of Egyptologists, Cairo: 28th March - 3rd April 2000' *Papers from the Institute of Archaeology* 11: 98-109.

Theroux, P. (1997). 'The imperilled Nile Delta', *National Geographic* January: 8-35.

Ucko, P. (1989). 'Foreword'. In *Conflict in the Archaeology of Living Traditions.* (Layton, R. ed.), London: Unwin Hyman, pp. ix-xvii.

Ucko, P. (1990a). 'Foreword'. In *The Politics of the Past* (Gathercole, P. and D. Lowenthal eds.), London: Routledge, pp. ix-xxi.

Ucko, P. (1990b). 'Foreword'. In *The Excluded Past: Archaeology in Education* (Stone, P. and R. MacKenzie eds.), London: Routledge, pp. ix-xxiv.

Ucko, P. (1992). 'Foreword'. In *Archaeological Heritage Management in the Modern World* (Cleere, H. ed.), London: Routledge, pp. ix-xiv.

El-Wakil, A. (1988). 'A brief report on the problems met with during excavations at Silvago, Delingat, Behera Governate'. In *The Archaeology of the Nile Delta: Problems and Priorities* (Brink, E. ed.), Amsterdam: Netherlands Foundation for Archaeological Research in Egypt, p. 265.

Wood, M. (1998). 'The use of the Pharaonic past in modern Egyptian nationalism', *Journal of the American Research Centre in Egypt* 35: 179-96.

Wunderlich, J. (1988). 'Investigations on the development of the western Nile Delta in Holocene times'. In *The Archaeology of the Nile Delta: Problems and Priorities* (Brink, E. ed.), Amsterdam: Netherlands Foundation for Archaeological Research in Egypt, pp. 251-7.

EPILOGUE

Niall FINNERAN

The present volume actually bears little relation to the running order of the conference on the day, although it is hoped that the underlying 'atmosphere' of the workshop has been retained; some contributions that were originally aired at the workshop have been modified to varying extents, whilst others have been specially commissioned when (for various reasons) original contributors were unable to provide a written version of their papers. For many reasons this volume has been much delayed in going to press, and sincere apologies are offered by the editor to both the contributors to this volume and those who attended the conference and expressed a desire for publication. I hope that the present work rewards their patience, reflects the ethos of the conference contributions and perhaps more importantly offers a thought-provoking contribution to the current debates surrounding the protection of Africa's cultural heritage *sensu lato*. For the record, here is the list of papers presented on the day (in running order):

1. Niall Finneran
   'Protecting archaeological landscapes: a case study from Ethiopia'
2. Charles Gore
   'A question of value: Nigerian museums'
3. Mohammed Mohammed
   'Rescuing Somali heritage'
4. Maitseo Bolaane
   'Heritage and wildlife in north-western Botswana'
5. Innocent Pikirayi
   'Landscape characterisation and cultural heritage management'
6. Peter Mitchell
   'Cultural heritage management in Lesotho'
7. Andrew Reid
   'Integrating African communities and archaeology'
8. Edwin Johnson
   'Problems and possibilities in Ethiopian codex conservation'
9. Patrick Darling
   'Conservation or con? The Nigerian/European experience'
10. Geoffrey Tassie
    'Egyptian cultural heritage: let's work together'
11. Alberto Larocca
    'Conservation of rock art in the Sahara'
12. Kevin MacDonald
    'A personal perspective on ethics and the African archaeologist'
13. Alinah Segobye
    'Commentary'

It is clear that the geographical scope of the workshop was considerable, as indeed was the subject matter, but to return to the '*sensu lato*' after the words African heritage above: the scales of definition ranged from the macrocosmic (landscape) to the microcosmic (Ethiopian codex). This appreciation of differential scales of analysis, placing the artefact on a equal footing with the 'site' or 'landscape' or wider social problem of antiquities looting, allowed for a varied and entertaining debate. The participants, thankfully, did not hold back from stirring controversy; ethical and legal points were aired openly, and as a whole -- as reported in a conference review by Jenny Doole of the Illicit Antiquities Research Centre, University of Cambridge -- some weeks after the event "the conclusion was cautiously optimistic" (Doole 2001).

Most importantly we sought to involve as many African participants as was practically possible. Again, the exigencies of time (and sadly economics) prevented the organisers from specially inviting participants from Africa, and paying their travel costs (we would hope to remedy this problem in any future conference), but fortunately we were able to turn to two exceptional visiting African academics, Drs. Pikirayi and Segobye, and importantly voices were also heard from African graduate students working at UCL and Oxford. It is a pity, then, that the final volume does not reflect (in terms of the African perspectives) the rich wealth and diversity of views presented at the workshop itself. As editor, I take full responsibility for this seeming lack of inclusiveness, and can only plead that I have tried my best to provide an open forum and opportunity for all those who wished to contribute to the final volume. I can only repeat, that on the day itself, both contributors and a challenging and appreciative audience mirrored the kind of diversity that the organisers of the workshop and strove to achieve, and perhaps most importantly a vigorous forum for debate was opened. Hopefully we can now maintain this momentum. The situation demands it.

The conference did not aim to give answers, let alone set itself up as a panacea for all ills. The key aim was to publicise; to highlight concerns in the protection of African heritage (however loosely it might be interpreted) and attempt to show some methodological and practical approaches that could be employed in order to help ameliorate the situation. A flavour of the papers as outlined above may be presented thus: area/country-specific case studies were discussed by Berte, Mitchell, Mohammed and Tassie; protection strategies for different kinds and scales of "site"/ "heritage"/ "artefact" were outlined by Finneran, Johnson and Larocca; possible interdisciplinary links and methodologies were offered by Bolaane, more reflective and generalised ethical and social concerns were aired by Reid and MacDonald. Most controversially (and this in the editor's opinion) the very thorny issue of the relationship between Nigerian museums and the illicit antiquities trade was tackled – from opposing ends of the spectrum – by thought-provoking papers from Darling and Gore, to their credit neither shrinking from some very unpalatable truths. Finally, overarching commentaries on the above issues were presented, from an African perspective, by Pikirayi and Segobye. In summary, then, a satisfying, stimulating and not uncontroversial programme; just how such a debate (in my own personal view) should be tackled. There is no room, when addressing such an important subject, for self-congratulatory academic backslapping. We have to be brutal when tackling unpalatable truths that in some cases may be exacerbated by our own actions, our own research. If we cannot provide concrete answers, then at least we need at least to be honest and open in our debate. It was generally agreed that it would be a worthwhile exercise to repeat this workshop in the near future and attempt to air a much wider range of concerns, involving workers from all backgrounds and walks of life who are connected in some way with Africa, but surely as archaeologists these are truly concerns that do affect us all.

Niall Finneran
Department of Archaeology
University of Southampton
December 2003

Reference

Doole, J. (2001) 'Conference Notes' *Culture Without Context* 8 (Spring 2001 online version).

CAMBRIDGE MONOGRAPHS IN AFRICAN ARCHAEOLOGY

No 1 BAR S75, 1980 **The Niger Delta** *Aspects of its Prehistoric Economy and Culture* by Nwanna Nzewunwa. ISBN 0 86054 083 9

No 2 BAR S89, 1980 **Prehistoric Investigations in the Region of Jenne, Mali** *A Study in the Development of Urbanism in the Sahel* by Susan Keech McIntosh and Roderick J. McIntosh ISBN 0 86054 103 7

No 3 BAR S97, 1981 **Off-Site Archaeology and Human Adaptation in Eastern Africa** *An Analysis of Regional Artefact Density in the Amboseli, Southern Kenya* by Robert Foley. ISBN 0 86054 114 2

No 4 BAR S114, 1981 **Later Pleistocene Cultural Adaptations in Sudanese Nubia** by Yousif Mukhtar el Amin. ISBN 0 86054 134 7

No 5 BAR S119, 1981 **Settlement Patterns in the Iron Age of Zululand** *An Ecological Interpretation* by Martin Hall. ISBN 0 86054 143 6

No 6 BAR S139, 1982 **The Neolithic Period in the Sudan, c. 6000-2500 B.C.** by Abbas S. Mohammed-Ali. ISBN 0 86054 170 3

No 7 BAR S195, 1984 **History and Ethnoarchaeology in Eastern Nigeria** *A Study of Igbo-Igala relations with special reference to the Anambra Valley* by Philip Adigwe Oguagha and Alex Ikechukwu Okpoko. ISBN 0 86054 249 1

No 8 BAR S197, 1984 **Meroitic Settlement in the Central Sudan** *An Analysis of Sites in the Nile Valley and the Western Butana* by Khidir Abdelkarim Ahmed. ISBN 0 86054 252 1

No 9 BAR S201, 1984 **Economy and Technology in the Late Stone Age of Southern Natal** by Charles Cable. ISBN 0 86054 258 0

No 10 BAR S207, 1984 **Frontiers** *Southern African Archaeology Today* edited by M. Hall, G. Avery, D.M. Avery, M.L. Wilson and A.J.B. Humphreys. ISBN 0 86054 268 8. £23.00.

No 11 BAR S215, 1984 **Archaeology and History in Southern Nigeria** *The ancient linear earthworks of Benin and Ishan* by P.J. Darling. ISBN 0 86054 275 0

No 12 BAR S213, 1984 **The Later Stone Age of Southernmost Africa** by Janette Deacon. ISBN 0 86054 276 9

No 13 BAR S254, 1985 **Fisher-Hunters and Neolithic Pastoralists in East Turkana, Kenya** by John Webster Barthelme. ISBN 0 86054 325 0

No 14 BAR S285, 1986 **The Archaeology of Central Darfur (Sudan) in the 1st Millennium A.D.** by Ibrahim Musa Mohammed. ISBN 0 86054 367 6.

No 15 BAR S293, 1986 **Stable Carbon Isotopes and Prehistoric Diets in the South-Western Cape Province, South Africa** by Judith Sealy. ISBN 0 86054 376 5.

No 16 BAR S318, 1986 **L'art rupestre préhistorique des massifs centraux sahariens** by Alfred Muzzolini.. ISBN 0 86054 406 0

No 17 BAR S321, 1987 **Spheriods and Battered Stones in the African Early and Middle Stone Age** by Pamela R. Willoughby. ISBN 0 86054 410 9

No 18 BAR S338, 1987 **The Royal Crowns of Kush** *A study in Middle Nile Valley regalia and iconography in the 1st millennia B.C. and A.D.* by Lázló Török.. ISBN 0 86054 432 X

No 19 BAR S339, 1987 **The Later Stone Age of the Drakensberg Range and its Foothills** by H. Opperman. ISBN 0 86054 437 0

No 20 BAR S350, 1987 **Socio-Economic Differentiation in the Neolithic Sudan** by Randi Haaland. ISBN 0 86054 453 2

No 21 BAR S351, 1987 **Later Stone Age Settlement Patterns in the Sandveld of the South-Western Cape Province, South Africa** by Anthony Manhire. ISBN 0 86054 454 0

No 22 BAR S365, 1987 **L'art rupestre du Fezzan septentrional (Libye) Widyan Zreda et Tarut (Wadi esh-Shati)** by Jean-Loïc Le Quellec. ISBN 0 86054 473 7

No 23 BAR S368, 1987 **Archaeology and Environment in the Libyan Sahara** *The excavations in the Tadrart Acacus, 1978-1983* edited by Barbara E. Barich. ISBN 0 86054 474 5

No 24 BAR S378, 1987 **The Early Farmers of Transkei, Southern Africa Before A.D. 1870** by J.M. Feely. ISBN 0 86054 486 9

No 25 BAR S380, 1987 **Later Stone Age Hunters and Gatherers of the Southern Transvaal** *Social and ecological interpretation* by Lyn Wadley. ISBN 0 86054 492 3

No 26 BAR S405, 1988 **Prehistoric Cultures and Environments in the Late Quaternary of Africa** edited by John Bower and David Lubell. ISBN 0 86054 520 2

No 27 BAR S418, 1988 **Zooarchaeology in the Middle Nile Valley** *A Study of four Neolithic Sites near Khartoum* by Ali Tigani El Mahi. ISBN 0 86054 539 3

No 28 BAR S422, 1988 **L'Ancienne Métallurgie du Fer à Madagascar** by Chantal Radimilahy. ISBN 0 86054 544 X

No 29 BAR S424, 1988 **El Geili The History of a Middle Nile Environment, 7000 B.C.-A.D. 1500** edited by I. Caneva. ISBN 0 86054 548 2

No 30 BAR S445, 1988 **The Ethnoarchaeology of the Zaghawa of Darfur (Sudan) Settlement and Transcience** by Natalie Tobert. ISBN 0 86054 574 1

No 31 BAR S455, 1988 **Shellfish in Prehistoric Diet Elands Bay, S.W. Cape Coast, South Africa** by W.F. Buchanan. ISBN 0 86054 584 9

No 32 BAR S456, 1988 **Houlouf I** *Archéologie des sociétés protohistoriques du Nord-Cameroun* by Augustin Holl. ISBN 0 86054 586 5

No 33   BAR S469, 1989 **The Predynastic Lithic Industries of Upper Egypt** by Liane L. Holmes. ISBN 0 86054 601 2 (two volumes)

No 34   BAR S521, 1989 **Fishing Sites of North and East Africa in the Late Pleistocene and Holocene** *Environmental Change and Human Adaptation* by Kathlyn Moore Stewart. ISBN 0 86054 662 4

No 35   BAR S523, 1989 **Plant Domestication in the Middle Nile Basin** *An Archaeoethnobotanical Case Study* by Anwar Abdel-Magid. ISBN 0 86054 664 0

No 36   BAR S537, 1989 **Archaeology and Settlement in Upper Nubia in the 1st Millennium A.D.** by David N. Edwards. ISBN 0 86054 682 9

No 37   BAR S541, 1989 **Prehistoric Settlement and Subsistence in the Kaduna Valley, Nigeria** by Kolawole David Aiyedun and Thurstan Shaw. ISBN 0 86054 684 5

No 38   BAR S640, 1996 **The Archaeology of the Meroitic State** *New perspectives on its social and political organisation* by David N. Edwards. ISBN 0 86054 825 2

No 39   BAR S647, 1996 **Islam, Archaeology and History** *Gao Region (Mali) ca. AD 900 - 1250* by Timothy Insoll. ISBN 0 86054 832 5

No 40   BAR S651, 1996 **State Formation in Egypt:** *Chronology and society* by Toby A.H. Wilkinson. ISBN 0 86054 838 4

No 41   BAR S680, 1997 **Recherches archéologiques sur la capitale de l'empire de Ghana** *Etude d'un secteur d'habitat à Koumbi Saleh, Mauritanie. Campagnes II-III-IV-V (1975-1976)-(1980-1981)* by S. Berthier. ISBN 0 86054 868 6

No 42   BAR S689, 1998 **The Lower Palaeolithic of the Maghreb** *Excavations and analyses at Ain Hanech, Algeria* by Mohamed Sahnouni. ISBN0 86954 875 9

No 43   BAR S715, 1998 **The Waterberg Plateau in the Northern Province, Republic of South Africa, in the Later Stone Age** by Maria M. Van der Ryst. ISBN 0 86054 893 7

No 44   BAR S734, 1998 **Cultural Succession and Continuity in S.E. Nigeria** *Excavations in Afikpo* by V. Emenike Chikwendu. ISBN 0 86054 921 6

No 45   BAR S763, 1999 **The Emergence of Food Production in Ethiopia** by Tertia Barnett. ISBN 0 86054 971 2

No 46   BAR S768, 1999 **Sociétés préhistoriques et Mégalithes dans le Nord-Ouest de la République Centrafricaine** by Étienne Zangato. ISBN 0 86054 980 1

No 47   BAR S775, 1999 **Ethnohistoric Archaeology of the Mukogodo in North-Central Kenya** *Hunter-gatherer subsistence and the transition to pastoralism in secondary settings* by Kennedy K. Mutundu. ISBN 0 86054 990 9

No 48   BAR S782, 1999 **Échanges et contacts le long du Nil et de la Mer Rouge dans l'époque protohistorique (IIIe et IIe millénaires avant J.-C.)** *Une synthèse préliminaire* by Andrea Manzo. ISBN 1 84171 002 4

No 49   BAR S838, 2000 **Ethno-Archaeology in Jenné, Mali** *Craft and status among smiths, potters and masons* by Adria LaViolette. ISBN 1 84171 043 1

No 50   BAR S860, 2000 **Hunter-Gatherers and Farmers** *An enduring Frontier in the Caledon Valley, South Africa* by Carolyn R. Thorp. ISBN 1 84171 061 X

No 51   BAR S906, 2000 **The Kintampo Complex** *The Late Holocene on the Gambaga Escarpment, Northern Ghana* by Joanna Casey. ISBN 1 84171 202 7

No 52   BAR S964, 2000 **The Middle and Later Stone Ages in the Mukogodo Hills of Central Kenya** *A Comparative Analysis of Lithic Artefacts from Shurmai (GnJm1) and Kakwa Lelash (GnJm2) Rockshelters* by G-Young Gang. ISBN 1 84171 251 5

No 53   BAR S1006, 2001 **Darfur (Sudan) In the Age of Stone Architecture c. 1000 - 1750 AD** *Problems in historical reconstruction* by Andrew James McGregor. ISBN 1 84171 285 X

No 54   BAR S1037, 2002 **Holocene Foragers, Fishers and Herders of Western Kenya** by Karega-Mũnene. ISBN 1 84171 1037

No 55   BAR S1090, 2002 **Archaeology and History in Ìlàrè District (Central Yorubaland, Nigeria) 1200-1900 A.D.** by Akinwumi O. Ogundiran. ISBN 1 84171 468 2

No 56   BAR S1133, 2003 **Ethnoarchaeology in the Zinder Region, Republic of Niger: the site of Kufan Kanawa** by Anne Haour. ISBN 1 84171 506 9

No 57   BAR S1187, 2003 **Le Capsien typique et le Capsien supérieur** *Évolution ou contemporanéité. Les données technologiques* by Noura Rahmani. ISBN 1 84171 553 0

No 58   BAR S1216, 2004 **Fortifications et urbanisation en Afrique orientale** by Stéphane Pradines. ISBN 1 84171 576 X

No 59   BAR S1247, 2004 **Archaeology and Geoarchaeology of the Mukogodo Hills and Ewaso Ng'iro Plains, Central Kenya** by Frederic Pearl. ISBN 1 84171 607 3

No 60   BAR S1289, 2004 **Islamic Archaeology in the Sudan** by Intisar Soghayroun Elzein. ISBN 1 84171 639 1.

No 61   BAR S1308, 2004 **An Ethnoarchaeological Study of Iron-Smelting Practices among the Pangwa and Fipa in Tanzania** by Randi Barndon. ISBN 1 84171 657 X.

No 62   BAR S1398, 2005 **Archaeology and History in North-Western Benin** by Lucas Pieter Petit. ISBN 1 84171 837 8.

No 63   BAR S1407, 2005 **Traditions céramiques, Identités et Peuplement en Sénégambie** *Ethnographie comparée et essai de reconstitution historique* by Moustapha Sall. ISBN 1 84171 850 5

No 64   BAR S1446, 2005 **Changing Settlement Patterns in the Aksum-Yeha Region of Ethiopia: 700 BC – AD 850** by Joseph W. Michels. ISBN 1 84171 882 3.

www.ingramcontent.com/pod-product-compliance
Ingram Content Group UK Ltd.
Pitfield, Milton Keynes, MK11 3LW, UK
UKHW061214180426
11947UKWH00029B/2037